THE BROTHERS KARAMAZOV was commissioned by Cincinnati Playhouse in the Park, the Repertory Theater of St Louis, and Otterbein College. The script's development was further aided by a workshop at the Playwrights' Center and a reading in the Mark Taper Forum's 1994 New Works Festival.

An earlier version of THE BROTHERS KARAMAZOV was staged by Otterbein College (Dennis Romer, Artistic Director, John Stefano, Chair, Theater Department), on 25 May 1994. The cast and creative contributors were:

FYODOR/MUSSYALOVICH/NELYUDOV/
DEVIL ....Geoffrey Nelson
DMITRI ....Todd Alan Crain
IVAN...Mark Von Oesen
ALYOSHA .... Ben P Sprunger
SMERDYAKOV/PLOTKINOV .... Ron Thomas
ZOSIMA/GRIGORY/SAMSONOV ....Adam Donmoyer
RAKITIN/PYOTR/PLASTUNOV...........Jason W Morrissette
GRUSHENKA ....Nicole A Franklin-Kern
KATYA/MARIA ....Jennie M Printz
FENYA/PORFIRY/STEPANIDA ....Jessica Buda
Ensemble ..Aimee Golart, Steve Lhamon, Yosvany Reyes

Director ....Ed Vaughan
Set .... Donna Williamson
Lights ....Fred J Thayer
Costumes...Katie Robbins
Sound .... Tamara Sommerfeld
Stage manager..................................Sarah Suzanne Hughes

The world premiere of THE BROTHERS KARAMAZOV, a co-production by Cincinnati Playhouse in the Park (Ed Stern, Producing Artistic Director, Buzz Ward, Executive Director), and the Repertory Theater of St Louis (Steven Woolf, Artistic Director, Mark D Bernstein, Managing Director), was presented on 6 January 1995. The cast and creative contributors were:

FYODOR/JUDGE/DEVIL/SECOND PRISONER Robert Elliott
DMITRI .... Michael Chaban
IVAN/FIRST CONSTABLE .... Michael Ornstein
ALYOSHA/SECOND CONSTABLE................Matthew Rauch
SMERDYAKOV/PLOTKINOV/FIRST PRISONER........ Ed Shea
ZOSIMA/SECOND PEASANT/MUSSYALOVICH/
NELYUDOV .... Joneal Joplin
RAKITIN/FIRST PEASANT/PLASTUNOV .... Paul Deboy
KATYA/MARIA .... Susan Ericksen
GRUSHENKA .... Katherine Heasley
FENYA/SAMSONOV/STEPANIDA .... Brooks Almy

Director ....Brian Kulick
Set & costumes..Mark Wendland
Lights ....Max De Volder
Stage managers .... T R Martin, Bruce Coyle

Thanks to the Ohio Joint Program in the Arts and Humanities and the McKnight Foundation for their generous support.

THE BROTHERS KARAMAZOV

Anthony Clarvoe

based on the novel by
Fyodor Dostoevsky

BROADWAY PLAY PUBLISHING INC
New York
www.broadwayplaypublishing.com
info@broadwayplaypublishing.com

Cover art compliments of Repertory Theatre of Saint Louis.

I S B N: 978-088145-695-0
First printing: November 2016

Book design: Marie Donovan
First published by B P P I in February 1997
Page make-up: Adobe InDesign
Typeface: Palatino

AUTHOR'S NOTE

This script got its start when Brian Kulick asked, "Have you considered adapting THE BROTHERS KARAMAZOV?" I started writing on the condition that Brian would direct the premiere and as many of the steps beforehand as possible.

The script was written thanks to Ed Stern, Steve Woolf, and Dennis Romer, each of whom gambled that there would be something to perform by the time his opening night arrived.

It never would have found its shape without the sharp dramaturgical eyes of Oskar Eustis, Susan Gregg, and Jeffrey Hatcher.

Its structure was influenced to an unusual degree by the work of Mark Wendland, a rare designer who thinks dramaturgically.

Ed Vaughan directed the earlier version with such lucidity that it was clear the script's infelicities were my problem.

It is a fortunate writer who can build a role on the gifts of a particular actor. I've been fortunate indeed with Katherine Heasley.

There would be nothing here, of course, without the father of the event, Fyodor Dostoevsky. Most of the dialogue and many of the scenes in this play are not to be found in his novel. A stance of passionately

patricidal reverence seemed truer to his great spirit
than dutiful fidelity would be. I hope some fraction of
that spirit made it into the script.

CHARACTERS & SETTING

The ensemble of seven men and three women play the following roles:

THE KARAMAZOVS

FYODOR, *fifties, a landowner and money-lender*
DMITRI, *thirty,* FYODOR'*s eldest son, a soldier*
IVAN, *late twenties,* FYODOR'*s middle son, a journalist*
ALYOSHA, *mid-twenties,* FYODOR'*s youngest son, a novice*
SMERDYAKOV, *late twenties,* FYODOR'*s bastard son, a servant*

THE MONASTERY

FATHER ZOSIMA, *fifties, the monastery's elder*
RAKITIN, *early thirties, a seminarian*

THE TOWN

KATYA VERKHOVTSEV, *twenties, an heiress,* DMITRI'*s fianceé*
GRUSHENKA SVETLOV, *twenties, beloved by* FYODOR *and* DMITRI
FENYA, *fifties,* GRUSHENKA'*s servant*
SAMSONOV, *fifties,* GRUSHENKA'*s patron*
PLOTKINOV, *a merchant*

THE INN AT MOKROYE

PLASTUNOV, *the innkeeper*
MUSSYALOVICH, *forties, an officer,* GRUSHENKA'*s first*

lover
MARIA, *a gypsy*
STEPANIDA, *a gypsy*
CONSTABLES

THE TRIAL

THE JUDGE
NELYUDOV, *the district attorney*
THE DEVIL

The ensemble also plays PEASANTS, VILLAGERS, *and*
PRISONERS.

SET

Chairs. A table. A window.

SCENE

Russia, 1860s. A small town in the middle of nowhere.

This is for Brian and for Kate.

ACT ONE

Scene One

(ALYOSHA *is kneeling.* FATHER ZOSIMA *stands watching.*)

ALYOSHA: A stone.

FATHER ZOSIMA: Yes, that's good.

ALYOSHA: In a river.

FATHER ZOSIMA: All right.

ALYOSHA: Completely inside the water.

FATHER ZOSIMA: Smooth stone? Craggy?

ALYOSHA: Getting smoother.

FATHER ZOSIMA: There you are.

ALYOSHA: But then I start noticing the current.

FATHER ZOSIMA: It's all right to notice the current. The world isn't a trap, Alyosha. Talk about the rock some more.

ALYOSHA: I start thinking, "Am I a big rock or a little rock? When the water flows over me, am I making a standing wave?" And by now all I can think about is the water, how the river is thoroughly full of water, bank to bank, solid liquid, and everything in it has water all over it, the grasses are stroked by water, every scale of every fish, it's a room made of moving water with a roof like beaten tin.

FATHER ZOSIMA: Alyosha—

ALYOSHA: And then I think how interesting it is to be thinking this, I've never thought of rivers like this before, I've only thought of them as a sort of emptiness with fish inside, when you look at a river your eye makes a cross-section, your eye makes a plane, your mind makes a moment, and another moment, but the river happens all at once.

FATHER ZOSIMA: This image may be too rich for you.

ALYOSHA: Try me again?

FATHER ZOSIMA: Very well. A stone. On a plain. No river. A great and empty desert plain.

ALYOSHA: Father?

FATHER ZOSIMA: Yes, Alyosha.

ALYOSHA: I'm already thinking of wind.

FATHER ZOSIMA: A stone. Underground. Far underground.

ALYOSHA: Father—

FATHER ZOSIMA: Yes, Alyosha.

ALYOSHA: Miners are digging their way toward me.

FATHER ZOSIMA: There are other ways to goodness, Alyosha.

ALYOSHA: Please, Father. I want to do this. Please.

FATHER ZOSIMA: Prayer isn't about wanting things, Alyosha. Prayer is about being completely with God. The moment you see yourself doing it, you're not doing it. From the beginning. What are we contemplating?

ALYOSHA: And the Lord said to Peter, "On this rock shall I build my church."

FATHER ZOSIMA: And the rock is?

ALYOSHA: Our purified soul.

FATHER ZOSIMA: And the church is?

ALYOSHA: The place we build in the world for God.

FATHER ZOSIMA: How do we build it?

ALYOSHA: Pray without ceasing. Lord, this is hard.

FATHER ZOSIMA: That's good. Start there.

(Above, RAKITIN ushers in FYODOR, IVAN, and SMERDYAKOV.)

RATIKIN: Father Zosima will see you in a moment.

SMERDYAKOV: Dmitri isn't here.

IVAN: Maybe he won't come. That would be fine with me.

FYODOR: Something lopsided about a place with no women in it.

IVAN: Father, if you start in—

FYODOR: Start in? Twenty-five saints here, saving their souls, eating cabbage and looking at each other. Not a woman in the place.

(A clock strikes.)

RATIKIN: Now, then, if you'll—

FYODOR: Right. Smerdyakov?

(FYODOR gestures to SMERDYAKOV, who holds out a tip for RAKITIN.)

FYODOR: Thanks for the trouble.

RATIKIN: Sir?

FYODOR: Hey, for the poor.

(RAKITIN takes the money. FYODOR, as he goes by, gives him a pat—)

FYODOR: Good boy. You look a little poor yourself, you keep that.

(RAKITIN *simultaneously gives a shrug and a nod, and pockets the money.*)

FYODOR: Thought so. Good for you.

(FYODOR, IVAN, SMERDYAKOV, *and* RAKITIN *cross down toward* FATHER ZOSIMA *and* ALYOSHA.)

FYODOR: Hey. Hey! My baby! Your sacredness, how do you do, Fyodor Pavlovich Karamazov, good to see you. Would you look at my cherub, look at him in the monk suit!

ALYOSHA: Hello, Father.

FYODOR: Ivan, look! Your mother to the life. He's a ghost with life in the face.

ALYOSHA: You're my brother Ivan?

FYODOR: Ivan Fyodorovich Karamazov, Alexei Fyodorovich Karamazov, Alyosha, Ivan, Ivan, Alyosha—my sons!

(SMERDYAKOV *clears his throat.*)

FYODOR: Not now. *(To* FATHER ZOSIMA*)* Is this a scene? Holiness? This is what a man lives for. Not you, of course. *(He prostrates himself.)* Bless me!

FATHER ZOSIMA: Don't try so hard.

FYODOR: You're good. *(Springing up again)* I was pushing. It's because I'm shy. God I could use a drink. Look: sweat!

IVAN: Father. Remember what you promised.

FYODOR: *(To* IVAN*)* Well, he's impressive— *(To* FATHER ZOSIMA*)* —you're impressive, someone thinks he's better than me and I say, all right, I'll be a clown. I've done it since I was their age, making jokes for my supper at nobleman's tables, now I'm a nobleman and I can't stop doing it. It's my tragic flaw.

FATHER ZOSIMA: I beg you not to be ashamed. That is the heart of all that troubles you.

FYODOR: Holy Elder, we need you. We need your connections to God. I know you're not a legal judge. I just want somebody near as possible to God to tell my son Dmitri that I'm right and he's wrong.

FATHER ZOSIMA: He is not here yet.

FYODOR: Late, typical. No respect for authority. *(To* SMERDYAKOV*)* You told him one o'clock?

*(*SMERDYAKOV *nods.)*

FYODOR: Have you got the notes?

*(*SMERDYAKOV *shows a sheaf of notes.)*

FYODOR: Got the document?

*(*SMERDYAKOV *shows the document.)*

FYODOR: Have you got the money?

SMERDYAKOV: You've got the money.

FYODOR: *(Waving a wad of bills)* Of course I've got the money! *(Holding it toward* FATHER ZOSIMA*)* Three thousand rubles. *(Snatching it out of reach again)* Oo! Sorry! Not for the collection plate! For my boy. I'll forgive him everything if he takes this and makes a fresh start on himself, if he tries to be good—

FATHER ZOSIMA: Let's wait till he arrives. Rather than have you try to prejudice me now.

FYODOR: *(To* ALYOSHA*)* I sent you to the right man. *(To* FATHER ZOSIMA*)* Alyosha's been a good boy?

FATHER ZOSIMA: We love him very much here.

FYODOR: He's the cream of the litter. And he'll rise, he'll rise—he's been all right?

FATHER ZOSIMA: Yes.

FYODOR: No incidents, no episodes?

FATHER ZOSIMA: None.

FYODOR: Good, this is a good place for you, Alyosha, good safe place. Should have put your mother in a place this quiet. *(Pulling* IVAN *forward)* This is my son, too, Reverend Father, my son Ivan—Ivan, ask for blessing—a writer, very advanced, ideas, full of them, all new. Tell the Elder one of those ideas, Ivan. That article—

IVAN: Really, though—

FYODOR: On the importance of religion.

IVAN: This is not the place.

(DMITRI enters.)

DMITRI: Forgive me. I seem to be late. Father.

FYODOR: Son.

(DMITRI and FYODOR bow to each other. DMITRI crosses to FATHER ZOSIMA and kneels for blessing.)

DMITRI: Reverend Father, pardon me please. *(He stands.)* And all of you…gentlemen. Help me. Who am I related to here? You're my brother Alexei?

ALYOSHA: Alexei Karamazov.

DMITRI: Dmitri Karamazov. Alyosha, I shall call you Alyosha—

ALYOSHA: That would make me happy.

DMITRI: And you must be my brother Ivan! Vonka!

IVAN: I prefer Ivan, actually.

DMITRI: Ivan. Alyosha. Look at this. I knew I had brothers, but I never felt it.

FYODOR: They've all come back to me. I want to say something. Sacred Elder, you have agreed to preside today, like the Solomon you are—

FATHER ZOSIMA: In a moment. We were discussing the writings of your son Ivan.

(Pause)

FYODOR: All right then. Ivan. Don't be shy—gets it from me—the article. The gist of it. You know the one—

SMERDYAKOV: The gist of it was—

(Everyone, startled, looks at SMERDYAKOV.*)*

SMERDYAKOV: The gist of it was that people only try to be good because they believe that Heaven and Hell are waiting. But he writes that word has come from Europe that God is dead, and Heaven and Hell are closed. So nothing is forbidden anymore, and everything is permitted: cannibalism, patricide. And finally—correct me if I'm wrong, Sir—if we truly do not believe in God we must live outside His law. We must live only by the Law of the Self, and find our Heaven or Hell on Earth.

DMITRI: Is that true?

IVAN: That was the argument I constructed.

DMITRI: I'll remember it.

FYODOR: *(To* SMERDYAKOV*)* You read all that? And with very good comprehension.

FATHER ZOSIMA: *(To* IVAN*)* You argue that there can be no goodness without faith. Do you believe that?

IVAN: I don't know.

FATHER ZOSIMA: You don't believe in your immortal soul, do you?

IVAN: I raise the question.

FATHER ZOSIMA: And it frets your heart. You divert yourself with arguments you don't believe, and you ache for an answer, and you fear the answer will come.

Thank the Creator who gave you a heart that can suffer so for answers. I pray you find a way to accept them into your heart.

(FATHER ZOSIMA *lifts his hand to bless* IVAN, *but* IVAN *crosses to him and kneels for blessing.*)

FYODOR: My boys. Seeing you together, for the first time in—for the first time. When they took you from me—maybe I was a little the worse for wear that day, maybe you didn't have your newest clothes on, maybe something broke. And in walk the in-laws. So I said take them. Raise them better than a man alone can do. Punishment of my life. But in my mind, we've always been together. My boys and me. Lounging around the table. Joking, roughhousing. Family. Maybe get some women in. Outside it's howling, but inside, we're warm, snug, a little bit lubricated…. A man's home. Sacred Elder, we have asked you to preside today, like the Solomon you are—

FATHER ZOSIMA: Mister Karamazov. May the young man speak.

(*Pause*)

FYODOR: Very well. Dmitri.

DMITRI: Reverend Elder—forgive me, I'm not educated, I don't even know how to address you—

FATHER ZOSIMA: Say what you need to.

DMITRI: He—Father—owes me money from my mother's estate. I want it now.

FYODOR: You always want money now.

DMITRI: It is my birthright. He's doled out a little over the years, a thousand at a time, but—I want my birthright.

FYODOR: You spend every kopek I send you. Throws it away.

DMITRI: I have reformed.

FYODOR: Into what?

DMITRI: I'm engaged to be married.

FATHER ZOSIMA: My blessing, young man.

FYODOR: Great, now he knocks up some camp follower.

DMITRI: The lady and I are unequal in fortune.

FYODOR: What does that mean? Is she some slut off the streets or what?

DMITRI: She's an exceptional person. I have given her my promise to reform my life. I need my birthright. She's rich.

FYODOR: You're joking.

DMITRI: She's an heiress.

FYODOR: Son! Come to my arms! You found yourself a fortune, that's marvelous!

DMITRI: No, I—I didn't know she was rich when I asked her—her father was ruined—

FYODOR: You didn't even know? That's marvelous!

DMITRI: And after that, after that her grandmother died and left her—

FYODOR: A fortune! You sensed it! Smelled it out! It's an instinct, inherited—a retriever, a golden retriever!

DMITRI: My God. I did something you think is clever.

FYODOR: It's the Karamazov breeding!

DMITRI: He thinks I'm a fortune-hunter!

FYODOR: How do you think I got that estate of your mother's? Through pluck and cunning the goatherd marries the princess. The end.

DMITRI: Is that what I'm doing? I didn't know that's what I was doing!

FYODOR: P S, he invests her money and makes a pile.

DMITRI: How can I look her in the face now.

FATHER ZOSIMA: Lieutenant—

FYODOR: Trust me, you won't have to for long. Now while she's hot for it, she'll sign over everything, marry her and you'll never have to look at her again! And then, Son—hey, you know I'm after somebody, too? Not for money, no, this time it's love. Agrafena Alexandrovna Svetlov. Grushenka. *(To* FATHER ZOSIMA*)* You know her? *(To* DMITRI*)* Wonderful girl, checkered past but lots of initiative. The fun we'll have! Huh? Huh? Father and son, out on the prowl.

DMITRI: I won't do what you did. I won't be like you.

FYODOR: But…I was proud of you there.

DMITRI: Just the money, please, my birthright, that's all I want—

FYODOR: Ivan, Alyosha, sorry you had to see him like this. But you boys and Papa can…. We can be a….

*(*IVAN *and* ALYOSHA *turn away.)*

FYODOR: What. Oh, what, then, you think he's right and I'm…. Dmitri. Listen. Now, you know all the money you've had from me has been in the form of loans. The total I've lent you—

DMITRI: Wait. Lent me?

FYODOR: Lent you. You signed a note for it every time. A promissory note. Smerdyakov?

*(*SMERDYAKOV *waves the sheaf of notes.)*

FYODOR: But listen, listen, here in this holy place I forgive you your debts. You hear me? I forgive you. Now—

DMITRI: How can you claim I owe you money? How can he claim that I—

FYODOR: And look. See? *(Waving the wad of bills)*
Three thousand rubles. For you, Son. A fresh start.
Smerdyakov.

(SMERDYAKOV *holds up the document.)*

FYODOR: You sign this, it releases me from any future
claims.

DMITRI: Three thousand—

FYODOR: That's right, no more humbling yourself by
mail. We can finally start to be a family.

DMITRI: But he owes me thousands more than this!

FATHER ZOSIMA: What is the worth of your mother's
estate?

DMITRI: I don't know for sure, a lot, he won't show me
the books.

FATHER ZOSIMA: How many thousands has he given
you?

DMITRI: I don't know, a few, I haven't kept track.

FYODOR: The total I've lent you now exceeds the worth
of her estate. You are in debt to me.

DMITRI: He's lying!

FYODOR: Prove it.

DMITRI: Is this a father? Tell me, please! How do I
honor this—thing, this—

FYODOR: You don't want to be my son anymore?
Fine. Who else have you got? You never had mothers.
(To DMITRI*)* Yours ran off with a seminarian with a
cough— *(To* ALYOSHA*)* Yours—remember when she
held you so close to the icons the candles lit your hair
on fire? *(To* IVAN*)* Remember the night she threw
herself in the river? Tell me about your mothers, go on,
all your lovely memories!

(ALYOSHA *gives a shriek of agony.)*

FYODOR: *(To* FATHER ZOSIMA*)* I thought you said he wasn't doing that anymore! He's his mother to the life. She was a screamer too.

DMITRI: You are an obscenity!

FYODOR: Fight me! Pistols! Three paces!

DMITRI: You Satan! *(*DMITRI *knocks* FYODOR *to the floor.)* Why does God permit you to exist!

FYODOR: Help!

DMITRI: Why did He let you ruin my life!

*(*DMITRI *throws himself onto* FYODOR. ALYOSHA *and* IVAN *try to hold* DMITRI. SMERDYAKOV *rushes to* FYODOR.*)*

IVAN: Stop it—

SMERDYAKOV: Sir—

ALYOSHA: Mitya! Stop this now! Now!

IVAN: You're both animals, kill each other if you want, just don't make me watch!

FYODOR: Did you see that? Sits on his holy ass while mine gets kicked— *(To* FATHER ZOSIMA*)* Did you notice that was happening? What are you going to do about it? Ha? What are you going to do to him?

*(*FATHER ZOSIMA *crosses painfully to* DMITRI.*)*

DMITRI: Please. How should I—what should I—

*(*FATHER ZOSIMA *holds out his hands for* DMITRI *to take in his own.* FATHER ZOSIMA *kneels at* DMITRI'*s feet, then bows to touch his forehead to the floor.)*

DMITRI: My God. My God.

FYODOR: What the hell was that? What the hell do you call that?

ALYOSHA: The love of God.

FYODOR: You think I've ruined your life. He thinks I've ruined…. This is the wrath of God. Smerdyakov. Three

thousand rubles. Take it home, put it under my pillow.
Go to Grushenka. Tell her it's waiting for her. Now
these notes. Dmitri's notes. Take them to Samsonov.
Get a receipt. Tell him to broker them for me. Whatever
he can get for them. Any buyer, I don't care who.

(SMERDYAKOV *exits.*)

FYODOR: Now I've ruined your life. Whoever buys
your debts will demand payment. You can't deliver.
You're a criminal. Whoever buys your debts will own
you. He can throw you in debtors' prison. A labor
camp. Send you to Siberia. And when your fingers
burn off in the cold, I want you to look at those
stumps and say, "When I had this hand, I used it to
hit my father." In church. (*To* FATHER ZOSIMA) This
is not a godly place! He is not here! And His servants
are thieving! You have stolen my chance to be good!
You— (*He points to* ALYOSHA.) Out of here today. Bag
and baggage. You— (*He points to* IVAN.) Come tonight,
we'll get drunk. You— (*He points to* DMITRI.) Go to
Hell. (*He exits.*)

IVAN: Excuse me, gentlemen. Reverend Elder, forgive
us. (*He exits.*)

FATHER ZOSIMA: Lieutenant. (*He points to* ALYOSHA.) I
will send this boy to you. Treat him gently. He is very
precious. And he is as much your father's son as you
are.

(DMITRI *exits.*)

ALYOSHA: We've exhausted you, Father, please may I
help you—

FATHER ZOSIMA: Alyosha. You must leave this place.

ALYOSHA: Father, no, I'll do better, let me stay and
learn from you, you are the father of my soul, I love
you—

FATHER ZOSIMA: Alyosha. This is going to be hard for you to hear. But no matter what you do, no matter how hard you work to remake yourself, your father is the father of your soul. This world is your father's property. It is your inheritance. I want you to take a long walk over your property before you give it up. Find work, make friends, find someone you love.

ALYOSHA: But why, when those things—you can hurt people, doing those things.

FATHER ZOSIMA: Go to your brothers. Go to your father. They are in terrible danger.

ALYOSHA: What can I do?

FATHER ZOSIMA: They need to see you listening to them. They are trying to be good. It is easier to be good if you know someone is listening.

ALYOSHA: When may I return here?

FATHER ZOSIMA: When I tell you.

ALYOSHA: But Father—

FATHER ZOSIMA: I'll tell you, Alyosha. You'll know. I don't have to be alive to do that.

(FATHER ZOSIMA *exits, leaving* ALYOSHA *alone.*)

(*The lights fade to:*)

Scene Two

(*Moonlight.* ALYOSHA *looks around him.* KATYA *sits at a table above, counting money into envelopes. A line of mendicant* PEASANTS *stands waiting. One by one they approach her, speak with her, receive an envelope, and exit.*)

ALYOSHA: Dmitri? Dmitri? Dmitri? Are you out here?

DMITRI: Shh.

(DMITRI *enters from the shadows, a bottle in his hand.*)

ALYOSHA: They said at your rooms I might find you here.

DMITRI: Shh. That's Katya. My fianceé. That's her.

ALYOSHA: Why are you out here?

DMITRI: Alyosha? Why did your elder bow to me?

ALYOSHA: I don't know.

DMITRI: He thinks I'm going to do something, doesn't he? Something bad. Look up there. She's the woman in the moon. Uh. Am I standing still?

ALYOSHA: Yes.

DMITRI: Feels like I'm falling backwards. Happens when I'm drunk.

ALYOSHA: Let me help you—

DMITRI: Falling and falling. Oh, mercy. I always thought that plunging from a height would have a grace to it. Like flying, only downward. But I'm batted back and forth by every wind I pass through, across this bottomless sky. (Holding out the bottle) Join me?

ALYOSHA: Let's go inside.

DMITRI: I'm sorry about this morning.

ALYOSHA: Why did you do it? The shouting, and you hit Father, why did you—I hate that—

DMITRI: I'm sorry. I'm a soldier. It's not a gentle life. (He gives ALYOSHA a bear hug.) But now I have a brother in this world! A good man!

ALYOSHA: Hardly.

DMITRI: No, I can feel it, the goodness comes off you, like a stove in the winter, I turn toward you I'm warmer. I'd never have met men like you and Ivan if that old Satan hadn't said you were my brothers. Ha! Think of that! Anyone could have stood in that room and I would have accepted him. What if someone

could introduce us all to each other? This is your
brother! How do you do? This is your sister! I see the
resemblance! Wouldn't that be something?

ALYOSHA: Dmitri. Mitya. I love you. You're a good
man.

DMITRI: No! Sometimes I think good thoughts—but I
do bad things. For a man to have the right thoughts
in his head and do evil anyway—that makes him all
the worse, don't you think? Our brother Ivan, now,
he thinks very bad thoughts, but he's pleasant to
everyone.

ALYOSHA: I don't think pleasant and good are the same
thing, Mitya.

DMITRI: You see! You're an expert in goodness. You can
tell me: All my life I've done bad things and said, well,
I'm a Karamazov. But you're a Karamazov, and you're
a virgin. The family's never had one of those before.
How the hell did a Karamazov become a monk?

ALYOSHA: One day I knew that I loved God and
believed in the everlasting life. The Scripture says, "If
thou wilt be perfect, distribute all that thou hast and
come, follow me." So I did.

DMITRI: You are a Karamazov.

ALYOSHA: What do you mean?

DMITRI: No half measures, especially in love. There's
a scorpion in our blood that goads us with this poison
of wanting whatever we can never get. (Holding out the
bottle) Sure you don't want some?

ALYOSHA: It reminds me of Father's breath. I do still
want things. My mother. I wish I could see her.

DMITRI: Everyone says she was a good woman.

ALYOSHA: And insane.

DMITRI: "I want my mother," he says.

ALYOSHA: It's childish.

DMITRI: Wounded men say it, in battle. Is that how you feel? Like you're in a battle all the time? Is that how it feels to be good?

ALYOSHA: I've never been in a battle.

DMITRI: If you were, I'd protect you.

ALYOSHA: I'll try to look out for you, too.

(KATYA *and a* PEASANT *come downstage.*)

PEASANT: Bless you, Miss.

KATYA: Please, no—

PEASANT: God in heaven will bless you for your charity.

KATYA: It is not charity. It is an investment in you.

PEASANT: Lieutenant! Young master!

KATYA: Mitya? Are you out here?

DMITRI: Just taking the air with my brother. My brother Alyosha!

KATYA: At last I get to meet you—

ALYOSHA: Good evening, I'm glad to—

KATYA: —come into the house, are you hungry, I can feed you—

PEASANT: Lieutenant, your fiancé is a saint.

KATYA: Oh, please.

PEASANT: A Christian saint, do you know that? Do you?

DMITRI: Yes, I do.

(*The* PEASANT *exits.*)

KATYA: I wish they wouldn't thank me so much. The only pleasure I've had from the inheritance is the chance to do some good.

DMITRI: It's hard to take something and give nothing back. Even thanks.

KATYA: I'd rather they gave me back themselves, improved.

DMITRI: Yes, I know.

KATYA: It's getting cold, do you want to—

DMITRI: Nothing, no, we're fine.

KATYA: There's only a few more waiting, then I'll join you.

DMITRI: You don't have to.

KATYA: I want to.

(KATYA *crosses above again.* DMITRI *watches.*)

DMITRI: What do you think a dog would do if he howled at the moon and the moon came down to him? He'd only try to gnaw it like a bone. Father thinks he ruined my life, but it was the wrong life anyway, the life I was reaching for, I see it now. She'll see it soon. Her father was my commander. We met at the ball he gave in her honor. His educated angel, home from the institute. I wasn't even supposed to be there. Nice girls didn't dance with me anymore. But Katya did.

(*Another pair of* PEASANTS *get their envelope from* KATYA *and cross down past the brothers.*)

DMITRI: Katya's out to reform Russia one greasy peasant at a time. That night she thought she'd start with me. And I thought, how dare she share the world with me, and be so pure.

ALYOSHA: But you fell in love with her, you love her—

DMITRI: Why did I think I could love another human being with my body full of Karamazov blood? And I thought I was being good! I didn't know what I was doing!

ALYOSHA: What were you doing?

DMITRI: What father does. She's better than me. So I had to ruin her.

(KATYA *and a* PEASANT *couple come down from above.*)

PEASANT: —and bless you again, Miss, bless you—

KATYA: Yes, thank you, no—

PEASANT: Are you her fiancé?

DMITRI: She's a saint, yes.

PEASANT: She's a goddess! Father Zosima gave us his blessing, but this! (*He holds up money.*) Bless you all!

(*The* PEASANTS *exit.*)

DMITRI: Is that the last of them?

KATYA: In there, yes. There is one more, though. Could you help me with it, Mitya?

DMITRI: What?

KATYA: I promised my aunt in Moscow I'd wire her some money. Three thousand rubles. She doesn't even need it really, but she was so good to me when father died. Take the three thousand. Wire it to Moscow. It's ridiculous Grandma left it all to me, I'll make Auntie take an allowance. (*She holds out the envelope.*) Take it. Take it with you tonight.

(DMITRI *takes it.*)

KATYA: Are you coming in?

DMITRI: We're fine out here.

KATYA: I'll get a wrap. I'll be right back.

(KATYA *exits.* DMITRI *throws the envelope at* ALYOSHA.)

DMITRI: Take this. Deliver it yourself. Take it!

ALYOSHA: What about Katya?

DMITRI: Do you know who ought to be with Katya? Ivan. They're right for each other. They think about the world. Alyosha? Do something for me?

ALYOSHA: What.

DMITRI: Tell Katya for me. Not tonight, let me get a head start, tell her tomorrow—the next day.

ALYOSHA: Mitya, I can't—

DMITRI: Brother, help me. I'll do evil here, I know it. Your Elder knew, that's why he bowed to me, wasn't it, to warn everyone. Tell Katya. Bow to her for me. Tell her I can never see her again.

ALYOSHA: Where will you go?

DMITRI: To the gutter where I belong.

(DMITRI *embraces* ALYOSHA. *He snatches the envelope and runs out.*)

ALYOSHA: Dmi—

(ALYOSHA *watches him go. Footsteps above.* ALYOSHA *runs out the other way.* KATYA *enters.*)

KATYA: Dmitri? Alyosha? Hello?

(*The lights fade.*)

Scene Three

(FENYA *is cleaning up the debris of an all-night card game.* GRUSHENKA *nurses a cup of coffee between her hands. One of the men passed out on the floor is* DMITRI.)

GRUSHENKA: Sit. Have some coffee.

FENYA: Just about done. Do you want anything from the kitchen?

GRUSHENKA: No. Do they have any of that bread? The egg bread?

FENYA: I'll see.

GRUSHENKA: Rest a minute. Oh, coffee is good. Take some beans, burn them, grind them, scald them. Look what they give you. Coffee is a good thing.

(DMITRI *stirs.*)

GRUSHENKA: And it raises the dead. Good morning, Lieutenant. I'm about to have breakfast, would you want some?

FENYA: Right. (*She rises with a sigh.*)

GRUSHENKA: Fenichka. Thank you. Have them pour some coffee for the Lieutenant? Tell them to put some brandy in.

DMITRI: Nothing for me.

(FENYA *exits.*)

GRUSHENKA: How much did you lose?

DMITRI: Nothing. The money I gambled with wasn't my own. So all I've lost is…everything. Well. Which is little enough to spend an evening in such charming company. Forgive me, I was not myself when we were introduced, Miss—

GRUSHENKA: We weren't.

(FENYA *enters carrying a tray.*)

FENYA: Egg bread.

GRUSHENKA: You're so good to me. Oh, this is good bread…

FENYA: Bread's good, I'm good, everything's good this morning.

GRUSHENKA: Morning is good. Share this with me, Lieutenant. Please. Or I won't enjoy it as much.

FENYA: Do as she says.

DMITRI: Thank you.

GRUSHENKA: Where do you go from here? Back to your regiment?

DMITRI: I don't have a regiment. I resigned my commission.

GRUSHENKA: Really, why?

FENYA: Not that it's any business of yours.

DMITRI: I thought I was getting married. But I'm not.

GRUSHENKA: So there.

FENYA: Eat your breakfast.

GRUSHENKA: I am. Are you going back home, then?

DMITRI: No.

GRUSHENKA: Where is home?

DMITRI: Here, maybe. Do you live close by? Do you think Plastunov needs someone to hold the horses? I didn't catch your name.

GRUSHENKA: I didn't drop it. I don't know yours.

DMITRI: No.

GRUSHENKA: Good to meet you.

FENYA: Oh, for—

GRUSHENKA: What?

FENYA: Stop playing with your food. You are such a bad girl.

GRUSHENKA: Not this morning. Everything is good this morning. Even me.

(SMERDYAKOV *enters, sees* DMITRI, *and freezes.*)

FENYA: What the hell do you want?

SMERDYAKOV: Oh. Hello. I'm here to get some fish. From Plastunov. Father—the master—likes a fish soup I learned how to make. I heard that Plastunov got a big delivery of fish. That's why I'm here. Well. I'll go get that fish now.

(SMERDYAKOV *moves to go.* DMITRI *springs on* SMERDYAKOV.)

DMITRI: Why has he sent you to spy on me!

SMERDYAKOV: I'll have a fit!

DMITRI: I'll break your legs!

SMERDYAKOV: I'll have a fit, I'll have a fit!

DMITRI: What are you talking about?

SMERDYAKOV: I'm an epileptic, Sir. Please be careful with me.

DMITRI: When did that happen?

SMERDYAKOV: It was after Father—the master—sent you away.

DMITRI: I didn't know.

GRUSHENKA: Do you know each other?

SMERDYAKOV: You haven't been introduced?

DMITRI: No.

SMERDYAKOV: I have to get home now. Bye.

GRUSHENKA: Who are you, Lieutenant?

DMITRI: My name is Dmitri Fyodorovich.

GRUSHENKA: Karamazov.

DMITRI: Yes.

GRUSHENKA: That's funny.

DMITRI: Not to me.

GRUSHENKA: Agrafena Alexandrovna Svetlov. Grushenka. Smerdyakov, why are you here?

SMERDYAKOV: Good question. A good question. Well. I had a message.

DMITRI: For me?

SMERDYAKOV: For Miss Svetlov.

DMITRI: From my father?

GRUSHENKA: Tell me the message.

SMERDYAKOV: No one is supposed to know but you.

DMITRI: Tell her the message.

GRUSHENKA: Go ahead.

SMERDYAKOV: My master says there is an envelope for Miss Svetlov. It is tied with a ribbon and sealed with three seals. Please don't hurt me, Sir. Inside it are three thousand rubles.

DMITRI: Three thousand—that should be mine!

SMERDYAKOV: And on it is written, "For my heavenly Grushenka, if she will come."

DMITRI: I'll kill him.

GRUSHENKA: Is that all the message?

SMERDYAKOV: Yes.

DMITRI: Liar! Tell!

SMERDYAKOV: Wait, yes, there is another thing. With all this money in the house, my master has taken to locking himself in at night. He's afraid someone might follow you, Miss, and break in when I open the door. So we have a signal. *(He knocks: tap...tap...tap-tap-tap.)* To say the coast is clear. That's the whole message.

DMITRI: Get out.

SMERDYAKOV: *(Backing out)* Please don't tell Father— the master—I let you know. He'd never trust me again.

DMITRI: Hey. Why do you keep calling him "Father"?

SMERDYAKOV: Do I? I'm sorry, slip of the tongue, I don't know who my father was, mother was the village idiot, funny how all our mothers are dead, he kills everybody, not that he's my father, she gave birth to me in his garden one night, that's all, but he's not my father, you're not my brother, no gentleman would mate with an idiot girl, no gentleman would admit to it anyway, though he might raise the child as some kind of servant, well, back to work, bye.

DMITRI: Smerdyakov? If Miss Svetlov knocks on Father's door and I don't hear from you before she crosses the threshhold, I'll kill you.

SMERDYAKOV: I'll bear it in mind, Sir. *(He exits.)*

GRUSHENKA: Really? My.

DMITRI: I didn't know you were that woman.

GRUSHENKA: I'm that woman.

DMITRI: Three thousand rubles.

GRUSHENKA: He'll go higher.

DMITRI: Are you his mistress?

GRUSHENKA: Why should I take his money in dribs and drabs, like you?

DMITRI: How do you know that—?

GRUSHENKA: If I marry him I'll get everything. My patron Samsonov is aging fast, poor thing. On our big nights, I help him balance his books. I have to make a change soon. I could tell your father I want to reform. He'd marry me. He won't live too long.

DMITRI: He's healthy. He's not very old. And he cares for nothing but himself. People like that live forever.

GRUSHENKA: Unless someone kills them first.

DMITRI: I say things when I'm angry.

GRUSHENKA: You do things when you're angry, too. Don't kill your father just yet, all right?

DMITRI: What do you care what happens to him?

GRUSHENKA: I don't. I care what happens to you.

DMITRI: Really? My.

GRUSHENKA: Every time he's given you money, he's made you sign a note for it, right? I know how he works.

DMITRI: I won't be owned by that man! I'll kill him first!

GRUSHENKA: You're not owned by your father. You're owned by whoever holds your notes. Your father sold them. At a discount.

DMITRI: Thank God, anyone rather than father, I'll find whoever bought them, we can arrange something, I'll talk to him.

GRUSHENKA: You are. Talking to him. Eat something, you look a little pale.

DMITRI: You paid my debts?

GRUSHENKA: I bought your notes. I've been buying a lot of gentlemen lately. It's a hobby. I've picked up a few men I might make a profit from. You I may have to unload. So don't kill your father just yet. Your exile to Siberia would badly devalue my property.

DMITRI: What will you do with me?

GRUSHENKA: He's hoping I'll send you to debtors' prison. Maybe I'll have all you gentlemen locked away.

DMITRI: Would you visit me?

GRUSHENKA: Of course. I'd have them bring breakfast like this. I could sit on the free side of the bars and look at you all. You could watch me eat.

(GRUSHENKA *chews a piece of bread as the lights fade to:)*

Scene Four

(KATYA *leads* ALYOSHA *in.)*

KATYA: Did he say anything about money? Three thousand rubles?

ALYOSHA: You know about that?

KATYA: I wired to Moscow. I know they never got the money. He must be so ashamed. But Alyosha—I don't care if he spent the money, he's ashamed, all right, if he wants to be ashamed of other people knowing, I understand, but why is he afraid of me? He told you.

ALYOSHA: I'm his brother.

KATYA: You barely know him! I'm his best friend in the world! Why can't he let me know him?

ALYOSHA: You know he went to some woman.

KATYA: Yes, well. That won't last. That's an infatuation. Does he think I care about that? That woman is an angel, did you know that? She's the most fantastic creature, she's beautiful, yes, but she's kind, too, and strong, and good. Grushenka? Come in to us. This is Alyosha. He's a friend.

(GRUSHENKA *crosses to them.)*

GRUSHENKA: She asked me to wait back there. Nice to meet you.

KATYA: We've just met, Alyosha, I asked her to come, I wanted to know her, I knew we'd work things out, everybody told me not to, but she came, and explained, and I'm so happy!

GRUSHENKA: She opened her door to me.

KATYA: And my heart, too. You should hear her story, Alyosha.

GRUSHENKA: You must be the kindest lady I've ever met.

KATYA: This is the sweetest woman! She's been through so much. A man—may I tell—

GRUSHENKA: Please.

KATYA: An officer, she loved him, and…everything. That was five years ago, he abandoned her, he married someone else. Now he's a widower, he's written, he's coming here, and she still loves the officer, no one but the officer, all this time. And he will come, he will, she will be happy again.

GRUSHENKA: I've never wanted Dmitri. You feed a stray and you can't get rid of it. Nobody wants to believe me but you.

KATYA: Do you know, the only other man she's ever… known is her patron, Mister Samsonov, the old man that…supports her, and he saved her life, he's more like a father. There's been no one else! No one! And for that she has this terrible reputation.

GRUSHENKA: Maybe if I'd had you before to defend me.

KATYA: I wish I'd known you years ago. There are things I've never been able to say to the people who know me, they don't—

GRUSHENKA: Not even Dmitri?

KATYA: Well, Dmitri, someday, but—look at this hand, Alyosha. It's so good. So good. (*She kisses* GRUSHENKA's *hand, three times.*) Look at her blushing! Isn't she sweet!

GRUSHENKA: You'll make me ashamed.

KATYA: Never be ashamed!

GRUSHENKA: I'm not as good as you think I am. I got Dmitri to notice me just for the fun of it, really.

KATYA: Poor old Dmitri!

GRUSHENKA: I did it to see if I could. So. Not so nice, am I.

KATYA: But now you'll save him! She's promised me she's going to tell Dmitri everything—how she loves this officer she's been waiting for—

GRUSHENKA: Did I say that?

KATYA: Didn't you? Of course you did.

GRUSHENKA: I don't think I'd promise something like that.

KATYA: I don't understand.

GRUSHENKA: You see? You open yourself up to me and I just want my own way. I'm sorry, if you say I promised, then I promised.

KATYA: Good.

GRUSHENKA: Yes. But now I'm thinking, what'll happen the next time I see Dmitri? I don't know. He wants me so badly, maybe I'll —I don't know—

KATYA: But just now you said—

GRUSHENKA: I'm just trying to tell you how I am. You're lovely, you're just—you kissed my hand. Three times. I'd have to kiss yours about three hundred times before we'd be even. You're so good, and so fine— she's lovely? Isn't she lovely?

ALYOSHA: Yes.

GRUSHENKA: He thinks so, too. May I? Please?

(GRUSHENKA *takes* KATYA's *hand in both of hers.*)

GRUSHENKA: Now your hand...your hand... *(She smiles.)* You know? I don't think I'm going to kiss your hand.

KATYA: All right. Whatever you like.

GRUSHENKA: Well, I think I like the idea that you kissed mine and I didn't kiss yours. I think it's pretty funny.

KATYA: That's—Grushenka, that's a little rude—

GRUSHENKA: It's damn funny.

KATYA: Maybe you'd rather leave.

ALYOSHA: Stop now. Please.

GRUSHENKA: Dmitri'll think it's a scream.

KATYA: Get out of here!

GRUSHENKA: All right. Oh! I think I have something of yours. Here. *(She holds out an envelope.)* It's a thousand rubles.

ALYOSHA: Please. Go now.

GRUSHENKA: Dmitri lost it. Gambling with me. I know he doesn't have money of his own. Is it yours?

KATYA: If you won it, it belongs to you.

GRUSHENKA: He threw it away, really. I've never seen a man try so hard to lose something. If he got it from you, it's not right for me to take it. Don't you think?

KATYA: You tell me. I've never taken money from a man.

GRUSHENKA: Well. You tell me. I've never had to pay for one.

KATYA: Bitch!

(KATYA lunges at GRUSHENKA, who dodges, laughing.)

GRUSHENKA: There we go.

KATYA: Slut! That was charity!

GRUSHENKA: Alyosha? Walk me home?

KATYA: That was charity! It was charity!

GRUSHENKA: I've got a story to tell you. *(She exits.)*

KATYA: I am a charitable person! I was trying to help him!

ALYOSHA: Stop, Katya—

KATYA: You try to be charitable! Look what happens!

ALYOSHA: Please, Katya, I can't—

KATYA: You try to be good. You try to be good.

ALYOSHA: Katya, I can't—listen to this, Katya, I can't—
stop—

KATYA: I'm better than this. I'm better than this. Good.
Good. Good.

(The lights fade.)

Scene Five

(Over the remains of dinner, FYODOR *and* IVAN *drink
cognac,* ALYOSHA *coffee.* SMERDYAKOV *stands by.)*

FYODOR: Only Alyosha comes to see me for unselfish
reasons. What was that reason again?

ALYOSHA: To find my mother's grave.

FYODOR: There we go.

ALYOSHA: You were going to show me where it is.

FYODOR: I've thought about that, long and hard, but
I can't for the life of me remember where I put that
grave. We laid her somewhere, I know that, but as for
where…. Well, I was distraught at the time. You know
us Karamazovs, when we're upset the first thing that
goes is our sense of direction.

ALYOSHA: I'll find it myself.

IVAN: I'll help you look, Alyosha, maybe the sexton
remembers.

FYODOR: Good idea, good idea, she'll turn up, I'm
sure of it. Boys, I'm glad you're with me. My soul is
troubled. God's truth, some mornings I wake up old.
Wait up enough nights for death to come knocking,
after a while you're old every day. Alyosha? Help me.

Tell me the truth. Are there hooks on the ceilings in
Hell?

ALYOSHA: What?

FYODOR: Are there? To hang the damned from? To
torture them?

ALYOSHA: No.

FYODOR: Truly? I've always imagined these hooks, iron
hooks. But then I think, how do they forge them? Do
they have an ironworks down there? Who mans it?
Demons? I want to know how it's run!

ALYOSHA: Not with hooks.

FYODOR: They must have some way to torture us.
I want to believe in the afterlife, but without those
hooks…. Don't deny me my Hell, Alyosha. Without it,
how can I ever be good?

ALYOSHA: You've been listening to Ivan.

FYODOR: It's true, I have, I admit it. Ivan, you've told
me that Alyosha must be either an idiot or a fraud.

IVAN: *(To* ALYOSHA*)* I never said that.

FYODOR: No. He's right, I'm joking. It's what you think,
though.

ALYOSHA: We shouldn't discuss this.

FYODOR: My soul is troubled. Alyosha, you've told me
if I listen to Ivan I'm damned for sure.

ALYOSHA: I never—

FYODOR: It is what you think! You think I'm damned,
don't you.

ALYOSHA: No.

FYODOR: You think I'm going to burn in Hell.

ALYOSHA: No.

FYODOR: Why not? Don't you want God to answer
your prayers?

ALYOSHA: I don't pray for that.

FYODOR: Know what you want.

IVAN: Stop it.

FYODOR: Know what you want!

IVAN: Father. Alyosha does not want you in Hell.
You're thinking of Dmitri. You never could tell us
apart.

FYODOR: You all want me in Hell. I'm afraid of it
myself. I'm afraid to believe in God. If there is a just
God, I'm in the shit. It's Him or me. Alyosha? Is there a
God?

ALYOSHA: Yes.

FYODOR: Yes? Look how sure he is. There really is?
And life everlasting?

ALYOSHA: Yes.

FYODOR: I believe you. My son. Look at his face. It
shines. I believe you. Ivan? Is there a God?

IVAN: No.

FYODOR: Ivan. Not even a little?

IVAN: No.

FYODOR: I believe you. My son—look at him—

IVAN: Shut up.

ALYOSHA: Father. Why do you do this.

FYODOR: I love you. Never forget that. We're father
and sons. We're doomed to love each other. Alyosha?
Would you pour?

(ALYOSHA *does so.* FYODOR *drinks.*)

FYODOR: Thanks. Mm! Delicious. Wait, though, this— this was water, before.

IVAN: What?

FYODOR: I'm serious, I've been trying to cut down, this was a pitcher of plain spring water, but now— Alyosha?

ALYOSHA: Stop it, Father.

FYODOR: It's a miracle!

IVAN: Stop teasing him.

FYODOR: Alyosha! Let me kiss the hem of your garment!

(ALYOSHA *screams once, briefly.*)

FYODOR: Got to you, didn't I? Tell me there wasn't a moment, huh? A tiny, teeny little moment when you wondered? A fraction of a moment of temptation to the most monstrous pride?

ALYOSHA: I was tempted, yes. But not that way. Sometimes, Father…you make it difficult to love you as much as I should.

FYODOR: Oh, God save me from Christian love. Christian love is like communion bread, it's flat and bland and this big around.

(FYODOR *makes a tight circle with his thumb and forefinger.* IVAN *laughs.*)

FYODOR: You're laughing at that? Have you ever loved anyone?

IVAN: Of course not.

FYODOR: Hmph. You haven't lived.

IVAN: Oh please—

FYODOR: You. Haven't. Lived.

IVAN: You're drunk.

FYODOR: No I'm not. All right, I am. I'm a general between campaigns. I'm an artist with inspiration and the paint store is closed.

IVAN: What are you drivelling about?

FYODOR: Love, you stick, what else does anyone drivel about? Love...it makes you think of the causes of things. How can I cause her to do this? How can I cause her to do that? Everything has a purpose: Maybe you can use it to get close to her.

IVAN: That isn't love.

ALYOSHA: It's seduction.

FYODOR: Call it what you like. The strategy's the same. It's all about wanting. That's the great thing. The want. Something's missing, a limb torn off me, first the shock, then the flesh screams, "Give me the rest of my body!" Everything hurts, air hurts, don't touch me don't wash me just stick her in place, stitch her down, make me whole again.

IVAN: And afterward?

FYODOR: Afterward what?

IVAN: I have to get out of here.

FYODOR: Try running away from it. See where it gets you.

IVAN: I don't know what you're talking about.

FYODOR: Bottle's empty. Time for bed. Smerdyakov! Help me!

(SMERDYAKOV *helps* FYODOR *stand and walk.* FYODOR *turns.)*

FYODOR: I'll tell you about afterward. You want to know what I'm scared of? More than anything in the world?

IVAN: Dmitri.

FYODOR: I'm scared that I'll never fall in love again.
That's what happens afterward. I think, if I stay with
this one, this is the last. There'll never be another.
The exhilaration that landed me here—never again.
Terrifies me. *(He exits.)*

IVAN: I love a lot of things. Stupid old—I love a lot of
things. Leaves, leaves are good. I love—it'll be winter
soon, trees bare, one day you notice they're covered
with buds, next time you think of them, leaves, tender
little pale green...it's stupid.

ALYOSHA: No.

IVAN: I like that it's stupid. Love from down here, no
brains, no cunning, just—like your heart is beating
outward, into—I don't know, everything sometimes,
those leaves, or faces, a crowd of people, they turn in
the breeze, you feel them tugging your chest.

ALYOSHA: You're halfway saved already.

IVAN: Or halfway damned. I hate a half-empty glass.
Who knows, maybe you'll save me. Maybe I'll save
you.

ALYOSHA: Go on.

IVAN: I want to go on living. I do. Drink the cup to the
dregs. I'll hang on till—I don't know—thirty, anyway.
Now that we're alone, I'll confess something to you. I
believe in God. Does that surprise you?

ALYOSHA: Are you joking with me?

IVAN: Like Father? No. I'm a reporter. I've seen things
that made me angry. Made me sick. Then things began
to make sense. The world made perfect sense for a
while, and I did some things that were...sensible, in the
circumstances. And after I...after I was better, I needed
to get away. Think.

ALYOSHA: What about?

IVAN: I'd covered a scene: parents, educated, well-to-do, five-year-old daughter found one morning locked in an outhouse, covered with bruises, face smeared with her own filth—by her father and mother, who slept like the just while she froze. Neighbors heard her in there, crying, beating her chest with her fist, praying to Father God. Brother, my godly novice, why did this need to be created? Whose fault is evil? They say we need knowledge of good and evil so we'll be free to choose between them. But I think the tuition runs a trifle high, don't you?

ALYOSHA: We'll see justice in the life to come.

IVAN: I want to see it. The martyrs' and the murderers' embrace. I want to see everyone learn why God made it so. If I'm dead, you wake me from my grave like a child on his Name-Day morning, you lead me to it. But. Tell me the truth. If you were designing the edifice of heaven, would you have built it on the tears of that little girl?

ALYOSHA: No.

IVAN: Would you accept that the people you were building it for had bought their heaven with her blood?

ALYOSHA: No.

IVAN: No. Eternal heaven is not worth the tears of that one little girl in that filthy hole beating her breast and praying to dear Father God. I can not forgive the torturer of a child. Who has the right to forgive someone else's suffering? And if I can't forgive, where's my place in heaven? I'm probably wrong. I don't care. It isn't God I don't accept, Alyosha. But heaven costs too much. I return my ticket.

ALYOSHA: You ask, who has the right to forgive? That Being does exist, He can forgive everything, everyone, He gave His blood for that, heaven is built on His tears.

IVAN: Christ. Yes.

ALYOSHA: Everyone's suffering happens to him. Do you believe that?

IVAN: Oh, yes. My icon of divine order is a Creator who brings a son into the world to live in poverty and neglect, driven through His Father's fallen world, hounded toward death, who in the end looks up and says, "Father, why have you forsaken me?" Oh, how I believe it.

ALYOSHA: And then He rises again.

IVAN: To sit at the right hand of the Father. No. No thank you.

ALYOSHA: You want justice against God.

IVAN: We know what justice is, you and I know. Why doesn't He?

ALYOSHA: He put the idea into our souls.

IVAN: So justice is our birthright. Do you think God the Father will give us our birthright, later, maybe, when he's done with the world? Don't you see we're all waiting for God's world to die so we can claim our birthright? Why not take it now? We're standing outside heaven like Dmitri in father's garden.

ALYOSHA: Is he out there?

IVAN: If he isn't he ought to be, with a pistol in his hand. If we stopped waiting, we could make our own justice, in this life. The only thing that stands in our way is our belief in these damnable fathers.

ALYOSHA: "If nothing is true, then everything is permitted." There's a name for this.

IVAN: Freedom.

ALYOSHA: Satan.

(A knock)

FYODOR: *(Off)* Grushenka?!

SMERDYAKOV: Sirs? If that is Dmitri Fyodorovich, please come to my aid? *(He exits.)*

FYODOR: *(Off)* Grushenka!?

(SMERDYAKOV returns with RAKITIN, calling:)

SMERDYAKOV: It's only a man, Sir!

RATIKIN: Been looking for you, cherub. Father Zosima's been asking for you.

ALYOSHA: What is it, what—

RATIKIN: He won't last the night.

ALYOSHA: Oh, no. Oh, my Heavenly Father, no. I have to go, I have to—I'm sorry, we have to talk some more, Brother, but—

IVAN: Another night.

(ALYOSHA exits.)

RATIKIN: Cold out there.

(IVAN shoves him a bottle of wine.)

RATIKIN: There's a crowd gathering. They've brought lanterns. So they can watch when he ascends into Heaven. What a country.

ALYOSHA: *(Off)* Misha?

(RAKITIN grabs the bottle and a plate of food.)

RATIKIN: Hey, for the poor.

(RAKITIN exits. SMERDYAKOV begins to clear the table.)

SMERDYAKOV: When do you return to Moscow, Sir?

IVAN: Why do you ask?

SMERDYAKOV: What an interesting place it must be.

IVAN: Say what you mean.

SMERDYAKOV: They're both insane, Sir, Father and Dmitri. Father at me every night, "Is she coming?" till midnight and after, and in the morning it's, "Why didn't she come?" as if it's my fault. Dmitri waking me up, shouting, "Hey! Did she come?" Now he's out there in the garden with a pistol in his hand? Sometimes I wish I could just die of the fright and be done. I wish I could have a fit. In fact I'm sure I will, tonight or tomorrow, a long one.

IVAN: What do you mean by "a long one"?

SMERDYAKOV: A long fit, Sir, they can last a long time— an hour or more, a day or two.

IVAN: I don't understand—are you saying you're going to stage a fit and lay low for a couple of days?

SMERDYAKOV: I might, I might, I'm so scared. If Dmitri does something, I might be accused as an accomplice.

IVAN: Why?

SMERDYAKOV: I let him know the signal, Sir.

IVAN: What signal?

SMERDYAKOV: Father locks himself in his room at night. I wait down here for Grushenka. He's afraid Dmitri will follow her here, and break in if I open the door, so we have a signal— *(He knocks: tap…tap…tap-tap-tap.)* — to say everything's safe.

IVAN: And you told this to Dmitri?

SMERDYAKOV: He was going to break my legs!

IVAN: So change the signal with Father.

SMERDYAKOV: And he'd ask why, and I'd confess, and he'd never trust me again, he'll kick me out of the house—

IVAN: If Dmitri comes and gives the signal, don't let him in.

SMERDYAKOV: And he'll think Grushenka's here, and do me an injury. I feel a fit coming on me. Father has an envelope with three thousand rubles in it. On it he's written, "To my heavenly Grushenka, if she will come." Dmitri knows that it's here.

IVAN: Stop it! Stop all this! Dmitri will not come here to kill father and steal his money.

SMERDYAKOV: He thinks that money is rightfully his. He knows that if Grushenka wants Father to marry her, he will. And she'll get everything. And Dmitri, and Alyosha, and you, Sir, will be out in the cold.

IVAN: So why do you advise me to go to Moscow, when you see what's happening here?

SMERDYAKOV: Exactly, Sir.

IVAN: Exactly what?

SMERDYAKOV: I like you, Sir. I'm trapped here. But if I were you, honestly, Sir, I'd get the hell away.

IVAN: Well, now that you mention it, I am going away in the morning—to Moscow.

SMERDYAKOV: Good idea, Sir.

IVAN: I've been meaning to for a while, I have business there that I've put off long enough.

SMERDYAKOV: You are a clever man, Sir. It always helps to talk to you.

(IVAN *crosses away.* SMERDYAKOV *lifts his tray of bottles and glasses. Lights up on* DMITRI. *Lights up on* KATYA, *reading a letter.*)

DMITRI: My Katya. My Fate. Tomorrow I will get money and give you back your three thousand rubles, and farewell to your fury, but farewell to your love, as well. I give you my word of honor, if I can't get it any other way, I will go to my father and smash his head

in and take it from under his pillow, the next time Ivan
goes away. Till then, I remain, your slave, Dmitri.

(The bottles and glasses rattle on the tray. The lights fade.)

END OF ACT ONE

ACT TWO

Scene One

(A crowd of VILLAGERS *kneels.)*

OLDER WOMAN: Father.

MEN: Lord.

ALL: Hear my prayer.

ALYOSHA: Grant rest to the soul of Father Zosima.

YOUNG WOMAN: May Father Zosima sit by your elbow.

RATIKIN: Father.

ALL: Father Zosima.

SICKLY MAN: Pray for us.

YOUNG WOMAN: Intercede for us.

ALL: Speak for us in Heaven.

YOUNG MAN: The Elder was good.

PREGNANT WOMAN: Good? He was holy.

ALYOSHA: Father Zosima was the bread and the wine of Christ.

ALL: A saint.

RATIKIN: Now his relics will be revered.

PREGNANT WOMAN: His body will never corrupt.

ALYOSHA: Corrupt? Impossible.

OLDER WOMAN: His body will perfume the air like myrrh.

SICKLY MAN: His relics will perform miracles.

PREGNANT WOMAN: Miracles this very day.

ALL: Father.

ALYOSHA: Let's not hope for miracles.

ALL: Sainted Father Zosima.

OLDER WOMAN: Send us a sign.

ALYOSHA: His goodness needs no proof by miracles.

SICKLY MAN: Heal me—

PREGNANT WOMAN: Let me touch the coffin—

YOUNG MAN: Ask God to forgive me for what I may do—

OLDER WOMAN: Let me kiss his hand—

ALYOSHA: Let us pray in silence.

(Pause)

RATIKIN: Do you smell something?

ALYOSHA: No.

PREGNANT WOMAN: Somebody smelled something!

SICKLY MAN: His body is holy incense!

OLDER WOMAN: The miracles have begun!

ALL: Holy of Holies.

RATIKIN: I definitely smell something.

PREGNANT WOMAN: I do too.

ALL: Sainted elder.

RATIKIN: Not a nice smell.

OLD MAN: Ha!

ALYOSHA: It can't be.

(People start quietly sidling out.)

ALL BUT A FEW: Father Zosima.

SICKLY MAN: Maybe it's a sign.

OLDER WOMAN: There is no sign, there is no smell.

ALYOSHA: Father Zosima.

ALL: Pray for us.

BOY: My God, what's the stench in here?

OLDER WOMAN: Shh!

RATIKIN: Whew!

ALL: Sainted elder.

RATIKIN: This is what happens when the church tries to manipulate the superstitions of the people.

ALYOSHA: Pray for us.

ALL: Holy one.

OLDER WOMAN: Will somebody open a window in here?!

(The last of the crowd disappears, leaving ALYOSHA *kneeling alone.* RAKITIN *crosses to him.)*

RATIKIN: Alyosha? You out here? Two hours I've been looking for you. What the—anybody but you, cherub, I'd say was looking angry.

ALYOSHA: Leave me alone.

RATIKIN: Huh! Got it in one. I'm surprised, I admit it, are you really so upset because your old man started stinking? What did you believe, he'd start working miracles the minute he croaked?

ALYOSHA: I believe, yes, I believe, I want to believe, and I will, all right?

RATIKIN: You are angry, but—don't tell me, oh, this is great, who are you angry at, God?

ALYOSHA: I'm not angry at God.

RATIKIN: Big of you.

ALYOSHA: I just don't accept His world.

RATIKIN: Uh huh. Have you eaten today?

ALYOSHA: I don't remember. I think so.

RATIKIN: Sure, a handful of bread maybe. I'd offer you something, but all I've got is some sausage from town, and I know you don't eat—

ALYOSHA: Give it to me.

RATIKIN: Hello! Boys, we have got ourselves a mutiny! You want to come to my place? I don't know about you, but I could use a drink.

ALYOSHA: A drink sounds good.

RATIKIN: Hoist anchor, boys, we're sailing to the Spanish Main!

ALYOSHA: I wasn't expecting miracles, you know.

RATIKIN: No…

ALYOSHA: I just thought—do you want some sausage?

RATIKIN: Take it, take it.

ALYOSHA: I just thought—then as soon as he died, he started to—

RATIKIN: Stink, he started to—

ALYOSHA: Like nature could hardly wait! Not even a day or two, any normal—but no, right away! Like God let nature insult him! Is there any more of this, I'm so hungry—

RATIKIN: Here.

ALYOSHA: I mean, where is the justice! The man was as innocent as a child. Why did God torture him like that? People like you and me, we can't expect justice, I know that, Misha, not in this life, but I guess I thought,

a man like that, couldn't God make an exception?
Not a miracle, not a revelation, just—did it have to be
shameful? Did it have to be complete humiliation?

RATIKIN: I know where, let's go.

ALYOSHA: I don't care.

RATIKIN: I thought I'd drop by Grushenka's.

ALYOSHA: Everyone laughed at him! I couldn't think of
anything to say—

RATIKIN: You want to come along?

ALYOSHA: I just stood there so embarrassed, why was I
embarrassed?

RATIKIN: Alyoshka.

ALYOSHA: What?

RATIKIN: You want to come to Grushenka's?

ALYOSHA: Yes.

RATIKIN: Really?

ALYOSHA: Let's go to Grushenka's.

RATIKIN: Yes! Raise the skull and crossbones, boys,
we're buccaneers now!

(ALYOSHA *and* RAKITIN *exit.*)

Scene Two

(*Lights up on* DMITRI *and* SAMSONOV, *who sits, leaning on
a cane.*)

DMITRI: Mister Samsonov, I have come with an offer—

SAMSONOV: I do not own your notes, Lieutenant.
Grushenka Svetlov owns your notes.

DMITRI: My offer concerns Grushenka Svetlov.

SAMSONOV: I don't own her either.

DMITRI: No, Your Honor, but everyone knows that you…employ…her. In your affairs.

SAMSONOV: What.

DMITRI: Business. Your business affairs.

SAMSONOV: And you want to hire her away?

DMITRI: Yes, no, not exactly—

SAMSONOV: As I do not own her, young man, I also do not rent her out.

DMITRI: God! This is—

SAMSONOV: This conversation reeks of obscenity, good evening, Sir.

DMITRI: I love her! She is the most extraordinary… being I have ever in the world, I've lost my, what, I've lost my—

SAMSONOV: Wits?

DMITRI: No, yes—

SAMSONOV: Heart?

DMITRI: I've lost my way, I've lost my—compass, wherever she goes, I just… I only want to face in her direction.

SAMSONOV: Lieutenant Karamazov, you're a very bad negotiator.

DMITRI: I know, she's told me.

SAMSONOV: She has a past, you know.

DMITRI: She's told me about you. How she thinks of you, she said, as more, at this point, like a father.

SAMSONOV: Is that how she thinks of me.

DMITRI: Well, look at yourself. No don't, I mean—if the word offends you—

SAMSONOV: In some contexts, the word father, as I'm sure you would be the very first to agree, can be deeply offensive, can it not, Dmitri Fyodorovich?

DMITRI: I see what you mean.

SAMSONOV: So I'm her father, your intentions are honorable—for a Karamazov that's a first—and you want me to—what?—give her away? Are you asking me to give you her hand?

DMITRI: Yes. Well, yes.

SAMSONOV: Well no. Not her hand or any other pound of flesh.

DMITRI: But why, Sir, please, you—

SAMSONOV: Because I don't own her! So I can't give her away! Can I! I'm tired, Lieutenant, why are you here?

DMITRI: You're right, Mister Samsonov. She has a past. And it's you.

SAMSONOV: In part.

DMITRI: And why I'm here—I am here to look you in the eye, Sir. I am looking her past in the eye and I am saying give her up. Give her up. And I will go to her and say, I have seen your past, I've seen what you've had to do to live until I found you and anything you had to do to live until I found you I count as a blessing. I know it's not what you wanted, I know you're ashamed, but I have gone to your shameful past and I have bought it off.

SAMSONOV: Well, that was harrowing.

DMITRI: I have a village. Chermashnya. I will deed it to you, all the land, all the buildings, the farms are productive.

SAMSONOV: Do you hold title?

DMITRI: My father holds it in my name.

SAMSONOV: If your father holds it, it's not in your name.

DMITRI: It belongs to me.

SAMSONOV: Not if your father holds it. What else have you got?

DMITRI: Three thousand rubles.

SAMSONOV: On you?

DMITRI: Yes, no—

SAMSONOV: Do you actually have any money?

DMITRI: My father—

SAMSONOV: Please.

DMITRI: It is owed me from my mother's estate! It is my birthright! I am offering my birthright!

SAMSONOV: You've given your birthright away! Don't you think I know that? The young woman is holding your debts, against my advice. If you want to give your birthright, you'd better get born a second time!

DMITRI: That is what I am trying to do! I offer you everything I'm worth.

SAMSONOV: That's nothing. You're in debt—less than nothing.

DMITRI: I would work for you. Set a term.

SAMSONOV: Seven years. Then seven again.

DMITRI: If you want.

SAMSONOV: I don't want. I'll be dead by then.

DMITRI: I love her. I know I'm offering nothing. Less than nothing. But that's all I am.

SAMSONOV: Young man. You finally made the right offer.

DMITRI: Sir, you mean you'll—

SAMSONOV: But you're making it to the wrong person. She's gone.

DMITRI: Where is she? I thought she was here, some— other room, I thought— *(He grabs* SAMSONOV's *cane, shouting:)* She said she'd be here!

SAMSONOV: She left ten minutes after she got here.

(Pause)

DMITRI: Father.

*(*SAMSONOV *laughs uproariously and exits as the lights change.* DMITRI *looks around, disoriented.)*

Scene Three

(A light in a window. FYODOR, *elaborately coiffed, sits in the window, looking up at the moon.)*

FYODOR: Oh, that's lovely.

*(*DMITRI *sees the lit window and his father in it, sighing with pleasure.* DMITRI *freezes.)*

FYODOR: Do some more.

*(*SMERDYAKOV *leans into the light and reads from a Bible.)*

SMERDYAKOV: A bundle of myrrh is my wellbeloved unto me; he shall lie all night betwixt my breasts.

*(*DMITRI *creeps toward the window.)*

SMERDYAKOV: Behold, thou art fair, my love; behold, thou art fair; thou hast doves' eyes. Behold, thou art fair, my beloved, yea, pleasant: also our bed is green. The beams of our house are cedar, and our rafters of fir. Chapter Two.

*(*DMITRI *knocks: tap...tap...tap-tap-tap.* FYODOR *starts and leans out the window.* DMITRI *shrinks back out of sight.* SMERDYAKOV *exits the window.)*

FYODOR: Grushenka? Is it you? Grushka! My goddess! Where are you?

(DMITRI *heaves a great sigh of relief.*)

FYODOR: I've got a present for you. You don't know how I've waited for this night! You've come!

(*A still moment. Then* DMITRI, *with a great effort, turns away.* SMERDYAKOV *enters.*)

SMERDYAKOV: Thief! Thief!

DMITRI: *(Turning)* Smerdyakov—

SMERDYAKOV: Patricide!

DMITRI: Quiet!

SMERDYAKOV: Patricide!

DMITRI: Shut up!

(DMITRI *strikes* SMERDYAKOV, *who falls to his knees.*)

SMERDYAKOV: Brother. No.

(SMERDYAKOV *has a seizure.* DMITRI *kneels by him, trying to hold him.*)

FYODOR: What the hell is going on out there! Smerdyakov! Smerdyakov! What the hell are you doing out there!

DMITRI: Dying. I don't know.

FYODOR: Who's out there?

(DMITRI *stands. The light catches his face.*)

DMITRI: Papa. I've come home.

(*Blackout*)

Scene Four

(GRUSHENKA *paces.* FENYA *enters, with* RAKITIN *and*
ALYOSHA.*)*

GRUSHENKA: Who's there?

FENYA: It's not him, Miss.

RATIKIN: It's me.

GRUSHENKA: Who's with you? Good Lord, you've
brought him.

RATIKIN: Get some candles in here, would you?

GRUSHENKA: Candles, of course, candles, Fenya, fetch
him a candle, would you? What a time to bring him!

RATIKIN: Aren't you pleased?

GRUSHENKA: I thought it was Dmitri breaking in.
Alyosha, you don't know how glad I am to see
you. I told Dmitri I was spending the evening with
Samsonov, my patron, doing the accounts. Fenya? Go
to the gate and watch for Dmitri?

FENYA: There's no one there, I just looked.

GRUSHENKA: Are the shutters fastened? Draw the
curtains.

RATIKIN: Why are you afraid of Dmitri? You can wrap
him around your finger.

GRUSHENKA: I'm waiting for news, precious news,
and I don't think he believed me, that I'd stay at
Samsonov's. He must be hunting for me at your
father's place, Alyosha. If he's there, he won't come
here, so much the better. Alyosha, you haven't said a
word. He's so shy.

ALYOSHA: My throat is sore.

FENYA: Is he sick?

GRUSHENKA: Are you sick?

RATIKIN: He's been crying.

ALYOSHA: If I could have something to drink.

GRUSHENKA: Crying, why.

RATIKIN: You promised me champagne, you know.

GRUSHENKA: Fenya, where's the champagne Dmitri left?

FENYA: Got it.

GRUSHENKA: Can you believe it, Alyosha, I promised him champagne if he brought you. I could use some myself.

RATIKIN: Is something the matter with you, too?

GRUSHENKA: My officer is coming. My man, my first, five years ago—you know, Alyosha, the lady told the story. He's at Mokroye, he wants to see me again—

RATIKIN: Does Dmitri know?

GRUSHENKA: God, no, he'd kill him. Five years, now he whistles and I'm ready to give myself to him again. What a cheap little heart I've got. To my cheap little heart. *(She drinks.)* Look at him looking. You are thirsty. You look so sad, Alyosha. Can't you smile?

(ALYOSHA tries to smile.)

GRUSHENKA: Are you angry with me about the other day, with the lady? I've been afraid you were angry.

RATIKIN: Now that's funny, you afraid of a cherub like him.

GRUSHENKA: You think it's funny 'cause you've got no conscience. Alyosha, when I ran home from the lady's, I thought, how he must despise a woman like me. I see you and I feel ashamed of myself. Just shameful. *(She strokes his face.)* Something to drink? Is that what you came for?

RATIKIN: He came to see you.

GRUSHENKA: Did you? Look then.

(Pause)

RATIKIN: Fenya, when you serve champagne, you're not supposed to open it in the kitchen, and it's not supposed to be warm.

FENYA: It's cold out.

RATIKIN: Honestly. Who else wants some? Alyosha, what'll we drink to? Grushka?

(ALYOSHA takes a glass, sips, and puts it down.)

ALYOSHA: I'd better not.

GRUSHENKA: Then I won't either. Drink it all, Rakitka.

RATIKIN: Very touching. He's grieving, what's your excuse? He's rebelling against God and stuffing his face with sausage.

GRUSHENKA: Why?

RATIKIN: His elder died today.

GRUSHENKA: I didn't know. Father Zosima—I didn't know, I'm—what am I doing? I'm sorry, Alyosha. I am, truly.

ALYOSHA: Rakitin? Don't mock me right now. I need you to be a little kind. Look at her—she took pity on me.

GRUSHENKA: Don't praise me, Alyosha, don't make me ashamed. I was so anxious to get hold of you that I promised Rakitin twenty-five rubles if he brought you. Fenya?

(FENYA holds out some bills to RAKITIN.)

RATIKIN: This is ridiculous.

GRUSHENKA: Take it, I owe it to you.

RATIKIN: As if I'd refuse it.

GRUSHENKA: Now go sit in the corner. You don't like us anyway, so be quiet.

RATIKIN: What should I like you for? What have either of you done for me?

GRUSHENKA: You should be good to people for no reason, like Alyosha.

ALYOSHA: I came here to be wicked, to find someone wicked, but—

GRUSHENKA: Don't you praise me.

ALYOSHA: I found a sister. A loving sister.

GRUSHENKA: I tied that lady in knots, I played with Dmitri, I toyed with your father—how can you call me your sister? I could finish you off right now!

ALYOSHA: No.

GRUSHENKA: I don't even have to do it. Let me just tell you. Listen to me. Hands. Fingers. You've got an imagination—

(ALYOSHA *puts a finger to his mouth to hush* GRUSHENKA.)

GRUSHENKA: Fingertips. Fingernails.

(ALYOSHA *puts the finger to* GRUSHENKA's *lips. She takes his wrist.*)

GRUSHENKA: Praise me now.

(GRUSHENKA *kisses* ALYOSHA *finger. He clasps her hand in his, fingers entwined.*)

GRUSHENKA: Here's the church.

(GRUSHENKA *moves their hands to a place mid-way up* ALYOSA's *cassock.*)

GRUSHENKA: Here's the steeple. Open the doors?

(GRUSHENKA *closes her eyes and tilts her face upward to be kissed.* ALYOSHA *holds her head in his hands.*)

ALYOSHA: Ope—open—open your eyes.

(ALYOSHA *and* GRUSHENKA *look at each other.*)

GRUSHENKA: He's a rock, this boy!

ALYOSHA: Yes, well.

GRUSHENKA: No, I mean—really. Really a rock.

ALYOSHA: Well. I've been practicing.

GRUSHENKA: Alyosha? What do I feel for my officer? Love? What?

ALYOSHA: You are so much more loving than I am! To want to go to that man and forgive him—

GRUSHENKA: Maybe I haven't quite forgiven him yet. Maybe what I've really loved all these years is my hatred. It's been such a support.

RATIKIN: I'd hate to be in his shoes.

GRUSHENKA: You'll never be in his shoes. You'll never in your life have a woman like me. Maybe he won't, either.

RATIKIN: Then why are you wearing the finery?

GRUSHENKA: Maybe I'll go to him—I was seventeen when he dropped me, skin and bones. Wearing this, I can sit by him, kiss him, and say, "Look at me. You know what I've become? Everything in the world you could want. Take a good look." Then I'll stand up and walk away.

RATIKIN: And afterward?

GRUSHENKA: Afterward what?

ALYOSHA: You don't have to go to that man. You could stay here.

GRUSHENKA: With you?

ALYOSHA: With my brother, Dmitri loves you—

RATIKIN: Dmitri's got no money. What can she do here?

GRUSHENKA: What can I—I can tear this finery off. I can send everything back to Samsonov tomorrow, all the presents, all the money. I can cut my face, burn off my hair, and sweep floors, and never get looked at anymore.

ALYOSHA: And just be listening.

RATIKIN: Like Hell.

(GRUSHENKA *throws the glass, which shatters.)*

GRUSHENKA: You think I couldn't do it? *(She picks up a piece of broken glass.)* The one who hurt me, all of them who hurt me, telling me they love me and tearing me up, they can fuck themselves, they'll never get me, never again!

(GRUSHENKA *puts the broken glass to her face, but* ALYOSHA *reaches swiftly and clenches his hand over hers.)*

GRUSHENKA: He had these perfect little moustaches, they moved whenever his mouth moved like a second smile, he played me songs on the guitar, he taught me to gamble, then he didn't want me anymore, I watched his mouth say he didn't want me anymore, his moustaches kept on smiling....

FENYA: Mister Karamazov. You're bleeding.

GRUSHENKA: Look what he's done. Look what he's done to us.

(ALYOSHA *and* GRUSHENKA *kiss. He holds her face in his hands.)*

ALYOSHA: Dmitri said something to me once. "What if someone could introduce us all to each other as brother and sister? How do you do? I see the resemblance! Wouldn't that be something?" Please. I've been alone all my life. Please may I have a sister in this world?

(ALYOSHA *and* GRUSHENKA *hold each other tightly.)*

RATIKIN: Thus endeth the lesson.

(Harness bells)

FENYA: My lady, my dear, my lady, it's the messenger, he's come. *(She runs out.)*

GRUSHENKA: What if I go to him. What if I take a knife along.

ALYOSHA: You won't take a knife with you.

GRUSHENKA: Won't I.

(FENYA enters.)

FENYA: It's a carriage from Mokroye, with a troika, they're getting fresh horses.

ALYOSHA: Grushenka. Listen.

GRUSHENKA: Why didn't you come to me before? Oh, my five years! I'm going. Fenya—

(FENYA and GRUSHENKA embrace.)

RATIKIN: So much for us.

GRUSHENKA: Good-bye, Rakitka, don't think too bad of me. Alyosha—

ALYOSHA: You have a brother who loves you.

GRUSHENKA: Tell Dmitri, bow to him for me, tell him to remember me, all his life, tell him I told you. *(She exits.)*

RATIKIN: Lovely. She ruins your brother and then tells him to remember it all his life. What a creature. He's a Pole, you know, that officer of hers. He's not even an officer now, I hear, lost his job. He's heard Grushenka's saved a little money, so he's turned up again.

ALYOSHA: She didn't take a knife.

RATIKIN: There are knives everywhere. So you saved Mary Magdalene? Cast out the devils? The miracles you hoped for started to come to pass?

ALYOSHA: Stop it, Misha.

RATIKIN: And you despise me now for those twenty-five rubles. You think I sold my friend. You're not Christ, you know!

ALYOSHA: I'd forgotten all about it—

RATIKIN: I'm not Judas!

ALYOSHA: You're the one bringing it up.

RATIKIN: To hell with you! To hell with all of you!

(RAKITIN *exits.* ALYOSHA *looks at his hand.*)

(The lights fade.)

Scene Four

(Moonlight. DMITRI *enters, his hands and shirt bloody.)*

DMITRI: Grushka! Grushka!

*(*FENYA *enters, holding a big kitchen knife.)*

FENYA: How did you get in here? Go away!

DMITRI: It's me, Fenya! It's Dmitri!

FENYA: I know who it is.

DMITRI: I just want to talk with her. Grushka!

FENYA: She's not here, Lieutenant!

DMITRI: Grushka!

FENYA: She's gone!

DMITRI: Liar!

*(*FENYA *holds up the knife defensively.)*

FENYA: No! I swear to God—

DMITRI: If you're lying I swear I... *(He grins at the knife.)* Lord. Granny, what big teeth you've got. Come on, Fenya— *(He sees her see the blood.)* What?

FENYA: Jesus. Look at the blood.

DMITRI: Oh. Nothing.

FENYA: What have you done.

DMITRI: Nothing, nothing much, nothing to worry over—

FENYA: What have you done to her!

DMITRI: Nothing, Fenya—

(FENYA *goes for* DMITRI *in a fury.*)

FENYA: What have you son of bitch done to her you tell me you bastard I'll kill you tell me I'll cut your throat!

DMITRI: Fenya, no.

FENYA: You killed her you killed her you—big hands, blood all over—

DMITRI: I love her, Fenya.

FENYA: Oh, God, he did kill her.

DMITRI: No.

FENYA: Caught her sled, dragged her out, wolf—

DMITRI: No!

FENYA: Wolf! Stick your face!

DMITRI: Fenya! Is she dead? Are you sure that she's dead?

FENYA: Whose blood is that!

DMITRI: Not hers!

FENYA: Whose!

DMITRI: A—dog—my father's—I went to look for Grushka there, he came at me, I hit him. Fenya. If I had killed her, why would I come here calling her name?

FENYA: She's alive?

DMITRI: Let's go find her.

FENYA: She's alive?

DMITRI: Let's go see. Is there anything I can clean up with?

FENYA: Your shirt's ruined.

DMITRI: I'll turn the cuffs under.

FENYA: Here, you don't—hold still. You know what she does that really gripes me?

DMITRI: What?

FENYA: She drops her curling papers all over the floor. Doing her hair?

DMITRI: Do you know, is Plotkinov's open?

FENYA: Think so.

DMITRI: I want to buy things to bring along.

FENYA: Takes them out, drops them behind her for me to pick up. You walk in, those curling papers rustle underfoot, they cover the floor, you kick them into piles, she's like a damn birch tree, ring of dry leaves all around her. White arms. There, that's better.

DMITRI: Come to Plotkinov's with me, I want to buy her everything she likes.

FENYA: I'm bringing the knife.

DMITRI: Fine.

FENYA: She'd better be alive.

DMITRI: Where are we going?

FENYA: I'll tell you when we get there.

DMITRI: Perfect. Plotkinov!

(Lights change as PLOTKINOV enters, laden with bottles, followed by a commotion of grocers.)

PLOTKINOV: The pastries and pate are loaded in the carriages!

DMITRI: Your boys are ready?

PLOTKINOV: They're fetching the instruments. What are we performing?

DMITRI: A rescue! Uh, Plotkinov…

PLOTKINOV: Your Lordship?

DMITRI: The pistols I…left with you.

PLOTKINOV: Still here.

DMITRI: I'll redeem them now.

PLOTKINOV: Yes, Your Lordship.

DMITRI: Right! Do we have enough torches!

(A shout from the band)

DMITRI: Yes! Now! Ladies and gentlemen? Let's be gone!

(Torchlight. DMITRI *looks up at lit windows. His grocers and gypsy women stand close by.)*

DMITRI: I wonder which window is theirs.

MARIA: I know which window is the innkeeper's, let's wake him.

DMITRI: Pray God hers is the one that's lit. Pray God they haven't gone to bed.

MARIA: Shall we let them know we're here?

STEPANIDA: Let's throw stones at the window!

MARIA: Yes! Find stones!

DMITRI: No, not stones, ladies and gentlemen, let's not throw stones at her, let's make a noise, a joyful noise, that's the way. Songs, not stones. Play music.

PLOTKINOV: Raise the torches, I can't see the strings.

DMITRI: Raise the torches. Ladies and gentlemen, look at us! We're a constellation!

STEPANIDA: What sign are we?

DMITRI: The sign of Karamazov! We hover over the birthplace of anyone born with desires too great for this world. Quick! Somebody! Rouse this house! Fire! Fire!

ALL: Fire! Fire!

(PLASTUNOV *pokes his head out a window.*)

PLASTUNOV: Fire? Who yells fire? Fire where?

DMITRI: Here! I am on fire!

PLASTUNOV: Dmitri Fyodorovich?

DMITRI: The same!

PLASTUNOV: Have you been giving champagne to the peasants again? The house is shut for the night, Dmitri, only a few of the lamps are lit—

DMITRI: Light them all! Set the walls on fire! Tonight everything should be made of light!

PLASTUNOV: Please don't—

DMITRI: What do you care if your house is standing tomorrow? Tomorrow is a vacuum, there's nothing in it but what it sucks out of today! Ladies and gentlemen, we'll break the doors down!

PLASTUNOV: Sir, no, I beg you—

(*Everyone stomps and shouts.*)

DMITRI: Play! Dance! Down with the doors! Down with all dead loves and all bad debts! Tonight all debts are forgiven. And all loves, all loves are forgiven, too. Play louder! Grushenka! Faster! Call her name! Grushenka!

ALL: Grushenka!! Grushenka!!!

(MUSSYALOVICH *leans out, bellowing:*)

MUSSYALOVICH: What the hell is this racket?

DMITRI: This racket, Sir, is Dmitri Fyodorovich Karamazov!

(The crowd laughs and shouts louder.)

DMITRI: Louder! Faster! Eat! Drink!

(GRUSHENKA appears in the window.)

GRUSHENKA: Mitya?

DMITRI: Grushenka! I've brought you everything good!

(The lights fade.)

Scene Five

(Lights up on GRUSHENKA, DMITRI, and MUSSYALOVICH sitting at a card table. PLASTUNOV hovers.)

MUSSYALOVICH: Who has openers?

DMITRI: Pass.

GRUSHENKA: Five rubles.

MUSSYALOVICH: I see it.

DMITRI: See it and raise it five.

GRUSHENKA: See your five and raise you five.

MUSSYALOVICH: See it.

DMITRI: What are the house rules, dealer? Any limit on bets and number of raises?

MUSSYALOVICH: This is only a friendly game.

GRUSHENKA: No limits on bets, no limits on raises.

DMITRI: That's what friends are for. See the five and raise you ten.

GRUSHENKA: Ten puts me even.

MUSSYALOVICH: Ten to me. I'll see it.

DMITRI: I hear you were stationed in Siberia.

MUSSYALOVICH: New cards?

DMITRI: Three. I hear almost nobody leaves there alive.

MUSSYALOVICH: You are thinking of the condemned. I was an officer. Cards, Grushka?

GRUSHENKA: One.

DMITRI: I hear you are an old...acquaintance of Miss Svetlov's.

MUSSYALOVICH: I am her first...acquaintance. Two cards to the dealer.

DMITRI: Trifon Borisich! Another bottle of the champagne, would you?

MUSSYALOVICH: Openers?

PLASTUNOV: Here you are.

GRUSHENKA: Ten.

MUSSYALOVICH: Your ten, raise twenty.

DMITRI: I hear you are an excellent cardplayer.

MUSSYALOVICH: You hear a great deal. You are newly acquainted with Miss Svetlov?

DMITRI: We are slightly acquainted. Ten and twenty and raise twenty.

MUSSYALOVICH: Forty to you, Grushka.

DMITRI: So when I got here, you two were...getting reacquainted?

(MUSSYALOVICH *chortles smugly.*)

GRUSHENKA: We were playing cards. Forty raise twenty.

MUSSYALOVICH: I taught her to play cards. His twenty, your twenty, raise fifty.

DMITRI: Hello. Trying to get rid of me? See your seventy—

GRUSHENKA: Wait. Trifon Borisich. You sold us a sealed deck?

PLASTUNOV: Yes.

MUSSYALOVICH: Grushka, what?

GRUSHENKA: Is this it?

PLASTUNOV: Ah. No.

GRUSHENKA: Pavel. Where did this deck come from.

MUSSYALOVICH: Am I accused—

GRUSHENKA: There. Yes. He's marked them.

MUSSYALOVICH: These are the cards I was handed.

GRUSHENKA: Yes. Perhaps. Many years ago.

MUSSYALOVICH: You accuse me—if you are not a woman I—

GRUSHENKA: Look, how…clumsily. He marked them. No one could ever play. An honest game. With these. Marked things.

DMITRI: Cash out.

MUSSYALOVICH: Pardon?

DMITRI: Cash out. You owe us nothing. Take your chips and go.

MUSSYALOVICH: And if I say no?

DMITRI: I brought pistols with me. We could share them.

PLASTUNOV: Please, not here, Dmitri, they'll close me, don't—

(MUSSYALOVICH *stands.*)

MUSSYALOVICH: A gentleman does not gamble with a man who does not know what he is risking. Come, Grushka.

(GRUSHENKA *is staring into space.*)

MUSSYALOVICH: Grushka. Come.

DMITRI: Now. What was the bet?

MUSSYALOVICH: Grushka? I come out of Siberia. To find you. Come now.

DMITRI: *(Counting chips)* Seventy to me, I think….

MUSSYALOVICH: Grushka.

DMITRI: And raise, oh, ten.

(DMITRI *drops his chips in the pot.)*

GRUSHENKA: This hand's tainted.

DMITRI: He was cheating us both.

MUSSYALOVICH: Grushka. I come across Russia. Out of Siberia. I see things there. I bury my wife. I bury everybody. I came back from there. You come with me now. Always the poker face, this one. I taught you that! I made you!

(GRUSHENKA *begins counting chips one by one.)*

MUSSYALOVICH: I taught her everything, does this one enjoy what I taught you? I love you!

GRUSHENKA: You taught me to know when someone is bluffing. *(She tosses chips in the pot.)*

MUSSYALOVICH: So cold so young. Better Siberia.

(MUSSYALOVICH *exits.* GRUSHENKA *watches him go, her hands clenched on the edges of the table to keep herself in her chair. She sobs again and again.* DMITRI *watches until she is silent.)*

DMITRI: What did you bet? What did you bet? You called and raised, how much did you raise?

GRUSHENKA: Ten.

DMITRI: Ten. I see you, and raise you twenty.

GRUSHENKA: You're crazy.

DMITRI: Keep it in mind, I'm crazy, I might have anything under here.

GRUSHENKA: Your cards are marked. I know what you have.

DMITRI: You have no idea what I have. The bet to you is twenty.

GRUSHENKA: Be crazy. That twenty and thirty.

DMITRI: Trifon Borisich!

PLASTUNOV: Right here.

DMITRI: *(Handing him a wad of bills)* Chips for this. Thirty, raise you fifty.

PLASTUNOV: I'll see if I—right away.

GRUSHENKA: Trifon Borisich?

(GRUSHENKA holds a wad of bills over her head, and he takes them as he passes.)

DMITRI: It's fifty to you.

GRUSHENKA: I know what it is. You didn't even have openers!

DMITRI: Mm-hm.

GRUSHENKA: You took three cards, for Christ's sake!

DMITRI: Mm-hm.

GRUSHENKA: You're crazy! You don't know the percentages, you don't know what money means!

DMITRI: I won't need money where I'm going. Fifty to you.

GRUSHENKA: All right! And fifty back! Where are you going?

DMITRI: It doesn't matter. Nothing after tonight matters.

GRUSHENKA: Why do you have pistols?

DMITRI: I thought they'd come in handy. Your fifty and one hundred more.

GRUSHENKA: Your hundred and one hundred fifty. Stop this.

DMITRI: One hundred fifty and two hundred more. You stop.

GRUSHENKA: And two hundred fifty. I'll stop if you will.

DMITRI: When the game ends we have to get up from the table. I never want to get up from this table. Five hundred more. I'll gamble till I'm cleaned out. Or the sun comes up. Whichever comes first.

GRUSHENKA: What if you win?

DMITRI: Huh. Hadn't thought of that. Five hundred more.

GRUSHENKA: You're raising your own raise, for Christ's sake!

DMITRI: Sorry.

GRUSHENKA: The bet is five hundred to me!

DMITRI: Right, yes, sorry.

GRUSHENKA: Five hundred. Raise you fifty.

DMITRI: Fifty?

GRUSHENKA: There it is.

DMITRI: See your fifty, raise you a hundred.

GRUSHENKA: You can't win! The point of the game is to win!

DMITRI: The bet to you is one hundred. Call me or raise me or fold.

GRUSHENKA: Like hell I'll fold! Your one hundred, raise you a hundred.

DMITRI: Yes! Your one hundred, raise you...

GRUSHENKA: You're running out of money.

DMITRI: Raise you twenty.

GRUSHENKA: Your twenty, raise you ten.

DMITRI: Don't pity me. Your ten, raise you ten.

GRUSHENKA: I don't do that. Your ten, raise you five.

DMITRI: See your five, raise you... *(He feels in his pockets and puts a bill on the table.)* Five.

GRUSHENKA: See your five— *(She feels in her bag and pulls out a handful of coins. She puts one on the table.)* Raise you a kopek.

DMITRI: A kopek?

GRUSHENKA: Maybe the sun will never come up.

DMITRI: See your kopek. Raise a kopek.

GRUSHENKA: And a kopek.

DMITRI: And a kopek.

GRUSHENKA: And a kopek.

DMITRI: And a... *(He has nothing left.)*

GRUSHENKA: Game over? Dmitri? Game over? You calling? *(Pause)* Can I lend you a kopek to call my bet? *(Pause)* Dmitri, when you've got nothing left to put on the table, the game is over.

(DMITRI stands. He steps onto the table. He kneels, arms wide. Pause)

GRUSHENKA: I'll see you.

(GRUSHENKA stands. With a sweep of her arm she sends chips and money flying. They embrace. Chips fly everywhere.)

(A loud pounding on the door)

CONSTABLE: *(Off)* Dmitri Fyodorovich Karamazov!

DMITRI: Not yet!

(More pounding)

GRUSHENKA: Dmitri, what—

(Everyone in the world comes in, behind two CONSTABLES.*)*

CONSTABLE: Dmitri Fyodorovich Karamazov!

DMITRI: That's me.

CONSTABLE: Come with us, please.

GRUSHENKA: Why? What are you doing with him?

CONSTABLE: There has been a murder.

GRUSHENKA: Who? Dmitri, what are they—

CONSTABLE: Fyodor Pavlovich Karamazov was murdered this evening.

DMITRI: My father is dead? *(A shout)* My father is dead!?!

(The lights fade.)

END OF ACT TWO

ACT THREE

Scene One

(Lights up on RAKITIN, *splendidly dressed in frock coat and top hat.)*

RATIKIN: That's a good question. I blame society.

(A crowd gathers around him.)

VOICE: Don't you blame Dmitri Karamazov?

RATIKIN: Certainly I blame Dmitri Karamazov for allegedly committing this crime, but I blame society, if you see what I mean, for committing Dmitri Karamazov.

VOICES: Mister Rakitin! Mister Rakitin!

RATIKIN: Yes, uh-huh?

VOICE: Why has this crime has become so notorious?

RATIKIN: It strikes a chord. It's a violent crime, we're a violent country.

VOICE: Compared with where?

RATIKIN: Certainly compared with Europe. We're a younger society. Look, some people don't want to hear this, but we are a nation of Karamazovs: violent, squandering, ruthless. We're the children of slaveowners. This country was built by the labor of serfs. That is our original sin. But that is how our pioneer fathers subdued this land. If we turn from those Karamazov roots, are we turning toward civilization? Or are we turning our backs on our strength, on our fathers, and what they built by the whip and the sword? Without that "original sin," who are we?

VOICES: Mister Rakitin! Over here! Mister Rakitin!

RATIKIN: You in the back. Yes.

VOICE: How can I meet Grushenka Svetlov?

(Laughter)

RATIKIN: Same as anyone, take a number.

(Hoots)

RATIKIN: No, no—

VOICE: Is she as attractive in person?

VOICE: How close are you?

RATIKIN: Let's just say she is very attractive and we've known each other quite some time. But you know? What most people don't know is, she really is a nice person. I have time for one more, yes, you've been waving.

VOICE: Do you see any hope for us?

RATIKIN: Well. It's scary, things are scary. What it did for me, and this was a shock, was make me see that if we continue to turn away from God, we're going to see a lot more of this kind of thing.

VOICES: Mister Rakitin! One more! Sir!

RATIKIN: Thank you, thanks. The book is *The Life and Thought of the Sainted Elder, Father Zosima*. The Bishop's introduction is wonderful. I'd be happy to talk with you afterward and sign your copy if you'd like, they tell me they're for sale in the lobby.

(They take their places in court.)

JUDGE: Lieutenant Karamazov. We cannot give you justice if you will not defend yourself. You say you are not guilty of this crime. But you seem bent on receiving the harshest of verdicts. Why is this? Lieutenant. We have no wish to wash our hands of you. Please try and save yourself.

DMITRI: That night was the great night of my life. My father. The man who destroyed all my chances. For years I had dreamed: how I'll pay him back. That night he stood in my arms' reach. A weapon in my fist. Do you know what I did? What I finally did?

NELYUDOV: Tell us please exactly what you did.

DMITRI: I listened—a moment—I'll never know why—

NELYUDOV: What did you hear?

ALYOSHA: Dmitri?

DMITRI: I heard.

ALYOSHA: Dmitri?

DMITRI: My brother's voice. Calling my name.

NELYUDOV: One of your brothers was there?

DMITRI: In spirit. That night he reminded me.

NELYUDOV: Of what?

ALYOSHA: Dmitri?

DMITRI: My name. My last and middle names are my father's. My first name, my Christian name, is mine. My brother called me by my Christian name.

NELYUDOV: Dmitri Fyodorovich. What did you do?

DMITRI: I looked at my father. And for the first time I felt: I am more than this old man's shadow. I am the brother—the brother in arms—of Alexei Fyodorovich Karamazov. Who will survive this world because he has worked so hard to forgive this man. And what I did…. Gentlemen, that night was the achievement of my life. I did not kill my father. I let my enemy live.

NELYUDOV: And then the servant Smerdyakov came out and you beat him half to death.

DMITRI: I never said I was blameless—

NELYUDOV: With the cane you stole from Mister Samsonov, later found bloody in the garden—

DMITRI: Yes—

NELYUDOV: You then proceeded to Grushenka Svetlov's and attacked her servant—

DMITRI: Yes—

NELYUDOV: You then ran up an enormous catering bill with the merchant Plotkinov, paid in cash you cannot account for—

DMITRI: All right! I'm a thug and a thief and a piece of scum. Thank you for reminding me.

NELYUDOV: Dmitri Fyodorovich.

DMITRI: I opened my ears to catch the voice of God and what do I get I get you!

NELYUDOV: Do you have anything to add?

DMITRI: No, that's it, that's my confession.

NELYUDOV: Dmitri Fyodorovich. That is not a confession.

DMITRI: I've confessed my soul to you.

NELYUDOV: You have not admitted to the crime.

DMITRI: I've admitted that I am a crime. That's enough.

(The court disassembles, leaving IVAN *and* ALYOSHA.*)*

Scene Two

(IVAN *and* ALYOSHA *stand, wrapped in their coats.*)

IVAN: Did you say something?

ALYOSHA: Is our mother buried here?

IVAN: Smerdyakov might know.

ALYOSHA: I'll ask him when he feels up to coming. I don't know why Mitya had to beat him half to death.

IVAN: I don't know why he confesses to that, but not to killing father. They'd lighten his sentence.

ALYOSHA: You think Mitya killed him.

IVAN: I think they'll convict him. Alyosha? Do you hate evil?

ALYOSHA: If I had a cancer that was eating me alive, I would hate that cancer. Yes, Ivan, I hate evil very much.

IVAN: What if a man were such a cancer? A man who is evil incarnate?

ALYOSHA: No man is evil incarnate, only Satan is—

IVAN: Only Satan is evil incarnate.

ALYOSHA: Forgive me, Ivan. Forgive what I said.

IVAN: And the sources of evil? Do you hate them too?

ALYOSHA: There is only one source of evil.

IVAN: Maybe so, but the local distributors do a hell of a job. A man who blights every life around him, the more dependent the better? Is that an evil man?

ALYOSHA: Yes, Ivan.

IVAN: Don't you ever wish that such men...stopped existing? I do.

ALYOSHA: Sometimes. It's a weakness. That wish is a sin in itself.

IVAN: That's my point, a man like that not only does evil, but infects with evil someone as good as you. Wouldn't you hate that man? If he had blighted the lives of children? Of his own children?

ALYOSHA: Why are you tempting me this way, Ivan? Why are you torturing me?

IVAN: Say it! If he tried to destroy his own children!

ALYOSHA: He's dead, Ivan.

IVAN: Say it! If you walked by a stableyard and saw children standing in ragged shirts, standing in their own filth, standing in all weathers—

ALYOSHA: He's dead! It doesn't matter anymore!

IVAN: And if those two children were anyone but you and me, if you could save them, if you could be their savior, if anyone could have saved us, Alyosha—

ALYOSHA: No! I know what you want me to say, and I won't!

IVAN: What won't you say, Alyosha?

ALYOSHA: You want me to say that I hated our father! I won't say it!

IVAN: Why not?

ALYOSHA: No! Sometimes I—

IVAN: Sometimes you'd look at him and think, if I had a weapon in my hand, I'd—

ALYOSHA: Why do you think I became a monk? So I would never ever ever have a weapon in my hand! (Pause) Don't make me say it, Ivan.

IVAN: You don't have to say it.

ALYOSHA: It isn't true.

IVAN: Only sometimes.

ALYOSHA: Only sometimes. My God, my God… Why have you done this to me?

IVAN: I was curious.

ALYOSHA: You were curious!

IVAN: I was curious to see if there was anyone in the world who was just like me. Where were you the night Father was killed?

ALYOSHA: At the monastery, why?

IVAN: Doing what?

ALYOSHA: My elder died that evening. I was lying in the headstones, grieving for him.

IVAN: All night? Every minute?

ALYOSHA: Yes.

IVAN: Could you prove that?

ALYOSHA: No. Why?

IVAN: No reason. You didn't kill him.

ALYOSHA: Of course I didn't kill him. Smerdyakov killed him.

IVAN: What? How do you know that?

ALYOSHA: I was gone, you were gone. Dmitri didn't do it.

IVAN: How are you so sure of that?

ALYOSHA: I just am. Smerdyakov's the only other one who was there.

IVAN: Father had a lot of enemies.

ALYOSHA: None like us. Who wanted to kill him as much as his sons?

(IVAN *turns and strides away from* ALYOSHA.)

Scene Three

(SMERDYAKOV *is lying down.*)

IVAN: Smerdyakov? Smerdyakov?

SMERDYAKOV: Sir? Over here, Sir.

(IVAN *crosses to* SMERDYAKOV.)

IVAN: Are you all right to talk? I won't tire you long.

SMERDYAKOV: When did you come back?

IVAN: Just this morning.

SMERDYAKOV: You missed the funeral?

IVAN: They couldn't get word to me in time.

SMERDYAKOV: What a shock.

IVAN: Yes.

SMERDYAKOV: Who could have guessed it would turn out like this?

IVAN: Well. You did.

SMERDYAKOV: Hm?

IVAN: You predicted all of it—even your fit.

SMERDYAKOV: Well, when you left, and I lost your protection—I was reeling, I thought, "It's going to happen, I'm about to fall!"

IVAN: I talked to a doctor friend in Moscow. He says you can't predict an epileptic fit. Though he says it is possible to fake one.

SMERDYAKOV: Ask the doctors here if the fit was a fake. Dmitri assaulted me with a weapon. Everything that happened that night I told to the district attorney.

IVAN: Have you told them about our conversation?

SMERDYAKOV: Yes. Not every word.

IVAN: Did you tell them that you told me you can fake a fit?

SMERDYAKOV: No.

IVAN: Why did you send me to Moscow just then? You knew there'd be trouble? You wanted to help me?

SMERDYAKOV: I told you to go as a way of warning you there'd be trouble. So you'd stay.

IVAN: Wait. You told me to go in order to get me to stay?

SMERDYAKOV: I thought you'd hear there was danger and naturally you'd stay to protect Father.

IVAN: Why didn't you say it directly? I told you I was leaving and you said, what, "It always helps to talk with a clever man"? Weren't you telling me you wanted me to go?

SMERDYAKOV: I was being ironic.

IVAN: Ironic?! Dmitri says you did it, that you faked a fit—

SMERDYAKOV: If I were planning to stage a fit, would I really have told you beforehand? I've never faked a seizure in my life.

IVAN: —that you faked a fit to give yourself an alibi and killed Father after Dmitri left.

SMERDYAKOV: Of course Dmitri says that. What do you say?

IVAN: All the evidence points to Dmitri, I'm afraid.

SMERDYAKOV: And not to me, you're afraid. Thank you very much.

IVAN: Why did you tell me you could fake a seizure?

SMERDYAKOV: I don't know, I was showing off. Everyone else in the family is good at something, all

I can do is make fish soup and alibis for Father. Now he's dead. Who am I going to cook for now?

IVAN: Look. I won't tell the police. All right?

SMERDYAKOV: I understand. And I won't mention our conversation.

IVAN: What do you mean? Are you threatening me?

SMERDYAKOV: All I meant is that you knew that something would happen to Father and you let it happen. People might think that if you're capable of that, you're capable of more. So why mention it?

IVAN: Are you saying I knew he was going to be murdered?

SMERDYAKOV: I'm saying you wouldn't haven't minded.

(IVAN *slaps* SMERDYAKOV.)

SMERDYAKOV: I'm sick, Sir! You shouldn't hit me!

IVAN: Stop crying. Stop it. What did you think, that I knew what Dmitri would do? That he and I planned it together? What?

SMERDYAKOV: I didn't know, I didn't know anything, why do you think I talked to you that night? I was trying to sound you out.

IVAN: About what?

SMERDYAKOV: About whether you wanted Father dead.

IVAN: You did kill him!

SMERDYAKOV: No. I didn't. You're a clever man, Sir, you know what happened. I'm so scared. I've been suspecting everybody.

IVAN: Very good. All right. We're sitting here talking. I haven't hit you again.

SMERDYAKOV: Thank you, Sir.

IVAN: I'm listening.

SMERDYAKOV: I had four ideas: One, Dmitri would kill him and you had no idea.

IVAN: Which turned out to be true.

SMERDYAKOV: No, you knew something was up, or you wouldn't have left. Two, you suspected Dmitri would kill him and you let nature take its course. That made sense, your hands would be clean and you'd get Dmitri's share of the inheritance when he was convicted. It's what a clever man like you would do, Sir. Three, you and Dmitri were in it together. When I thought of that, I almost had a fit on the spot.

IVAN: Why?

SMERDYAKOV: Because if you and Dmitri are in it together, I'm sunk. You'd plan it so I'd be blamed. And look what he's telling people now! Look how you come here accusing me! The reason I told you I could fake a fit, Sir? The real reason was so you'd know I could give myself an alibi. So you couldn't pin it on me.

IVAN: You said four ideas. What's the fourth?

SMERDYAKOV: You wanted me to do it.

IVAN: What?

SMERDYAKOV: You wanted me to kill Father.

IVAN: What on Earth could possibly make you think I wanted that?

SMERDYAKOV: Our conversation.

IVAN: I never told you to kill him, you never told me you'd kill him, nobody said anything about killing him, nobody said anything about anything, it was just a weird conversation about maybe something's going to happen to Father. A very weird conversation.

SMERDYAKOV: Did you mention it to him?

IVAN: What?

SMERDYAKOV: Our conversation. Did you ever say, "Hey, old man, I just had the weirdest talk with funny old Smerdyakov, he was ranting on and on, all scared something bad's about to happen to you. Say, you know? Think I'll go to Moscow now. Bye." Ever tell him something like that?

IVAN: No.

SMERDYAKOV: No. And since you didn't see fit to mention it to him, I haven't seen fit to tell the police.

IVAN: I had nothing to do with Father's death.

SMERDYAKOV: How awkward to have to keep saying that.

(IVAN *crosses away from* SMERDYAKOV.)

Scene Four

(IVAN *joins* KATYA, *who holds a letter.*)

KATYA: What can I do? He says it all, right here.

IVAN: Sometimes… Sometimes, Miss Verkhovtsev, people say things they don't mean.

KATYA: *(Reading)* "Tomorrow I will get money and give you back your three thousand rubles, and farewell to your fury, but farewell to your love, as well. I give you my word of honor, if I can't get it any other way, I will go to my father and smash his head in and take it from under his pillow, the next time Ivan goes away—"

IVAN: When did he write this?

KATYA: I received it the day of the murder. Are you saying he didn't mean this?

IVAN: People mean things at the moment they say them, maybe, or they say them along with a lot of other things, to see which one sounds the most like how they feel. It's trial and error. Dmitri is trial and error all the time.

KATYA: You're defending him.

IVAN: Am I? All right, then, I am. It's something I'm trying. I've condemned him long enough, now I want to try the other way.

KATYA: In the face of a statement like this?

IVAN: Because of a statement like this! I know what this means! I recognize this!

KATYA: It means what it says. He was planning to kill his father.

IVAN: Don't you see? He says here he can kill his father!

KATYA: Yes! And now he's done it.

IVAN: No!

KATYA: Why not?

IVAN: Because he didn't have to!

KATYA: Why not?

IVAN: Because he said right here that he could! He said it to you, to his conscience, precisely so that he wouldn't have to do it! He puts it into words. He takes the wish and instead of putting it into action, he puts it into words!

KATYA: What kind of a person. Has to think like that.

IVAN: A person who knows he has evil inside him. Dmitri. Alyosha. Me.

KATYA: Can't people say what they mean and...mean what they say and do what they say they are going to do....

IVAN: I wouldn't know. I'm a Karamazov.

KATYA: I love Dmitri. I have said it a thousand times.

IVAN: Is it true?

KATYA: I heard him today. Asking his lawyer if a woman can join her man in Siberia if he's convicted. Her man. He loves her. So that's Love now. Here. In my heart. There's an icon in my heart. The two of them. When I kneel by my bed and try to pray, to look into my heart, I see them. It must be wonderful to be a Karamazov, and be desperate for one thing one minute and desperate for something else the next.

IVAN: Miss Verkhovtsev. Katya. You hold him in your hands. You can save him or destroy him.

KATYA: *(Holding the letter)* He's already destroyed himself.

IVAN: Give whatever evidence you want tomorrow. I don't care.

KATYA: I'll be under oath.

IVAN: "So help me God." Really? Katya. Really?

KATYA: I cannot forgive this. It is who I am. I will never change. This is my heart. I will not let any of it, any of it, any of it go. Never.

(Someone applauds. IVAN *turns and gives a startled cry. A nattily dressed gentleman enters. He has* FYODOR KARAMAZOV's *face. He also has horns on his forehead* KATYA *does not see him.)*

KATYA: Mister Karamazov, what—?

IVAN: Nothing. It's just—nothing, but—listen.

DEVIL: Evening, Ivan.

KATYA: Mister Karamazov? Ivan? What's the matter?

(The DEVIL *exits.)*

IVAN: Dmitri is a fool and a thief and a murderer. He is no one to make you pass judgment on yourself. Katya. Believe me. You can't do this. You can't live like this. It'll kill you.

KATYA: Let it try. See what happens.

IVAN: Believe me.

(IVAN *runs out.* KATYA *watches him go.*)

NELYUDOV: Miss Verkhovtsev.

(KATYA *is in court.*)

NELYUDOV: The night of the murder the defendant squandered vast sums of money.

KATYA: He did not steal that money from his father. He got it from me.

NELYUDOV: Stolen?

KATYA: No. I gave it to him.

DMITRI: Katya, no!

JUDGE: Order.

DMITRI: Don't do this, Katya, don't make me take this from you—

JUDGE: Silence!

KATYA: I knew he would never accept a loan from me. I gave him the money to take care of for me, so he would have it to use if he needed it, and he would not need to....

NELYUDOV: Would not need to rob his father?

KATYA: No! I could see how he hated to—

NELYUDOV: How he hated his father.

KATYA: No! I could see how he hated to need his father's money. I had the money, we were engaged, why shouldn't I—

NELYUDOV: Some would call it improper—

KATYA: Damn propriety! Charity is the opposite of propriety. Charity is the giving of freedom. That is why I gave Dmitri the money. I wanted to free him from his past. So he would no longer need his father, and he would—

NELYUDOV: And he would need you instead.

KATYA: Perhaps. So.

NELYUDOV: Thank you, Miss Verkhovtsev. This is the most powerful motive we have yet heard. The very night he took your money, he spent every kopek in the fleshpots of Mokroye. Then, to repay this debt of shame, he robbed his father two weeks later! Then, helpless to resist his base desires, he went to Mokroye and spent his father's money as well!

KATYA: You are wrong! I can prove it.

NELYUDOV: I am sorry, a woman's pride can scarcely bear—

KATYA: That he gave my money to Grushenka Svetlov. I know. She came to my house and returned it to me. One thousand rubles. Leaving two thousand to spend on the night of the murder. Not his father's money. Mine.

NELYUDOV: The court will bear in mind that the witness is prejudiced toward her fiancé.

KATYA: I am not. His fiancée, anymore. Gentlemen, the man is not a thief. Everything he has, the man throws away.

NELYUDOV: One more question, Miss Verkhovtsev. Have you ever heard the defendant issue threats against his father?

DMITRI: Katya, tell them the truth.

JUDGE: Order.

(Pause)

KATYA: I never heard him. Do that. Threaten him. No.

(The court disassembles, leaving DMITRI.)

Scene Five

(GRUSHENKA stands at a distance from DMITRI.)

GRUSHENKA: I'm used to the snickering. I am. I'm used to the staring. They were very attentive in court, weren't they? Very tolerant of me? Very polite and open-minded. Bastards, evil, evil—I'm used to it. I'm used to all of it. I'm not used to so much of it at once.

DMITRI: Do you think I did it?

GRUSHENKA: I've told you this. What did I say on the stand today? Why can't you believe me? *(Pause)* Could you believe my officer today? The outraged dignity of the Polish nation. He writes to me every day now, asking for money. I saw him in the corridor this morning, I slipped him five rubles for something to eat so he wouldn't pass out on the witness stand.

DMITRI: You're giving him money.

GRUSHENKA: Mitya. That night I think I was going to murder him. I didn't come there planning to do it. Alyosha helped me. But once I was there...those cards of his, and...what he said to me... I thought, I can go with him to his room now and that's where I'll murder him. If you hadn't been there, nothing would have kept me at that table. You kept me playing. That's what you did that night. If you're guilty, so am I. We thought we needed those old men dead. But we didn't. Mitya. We didn't. We found something better to do.

(IVAN and ALYOSHA enter.)

IVAN: *(To ALYOSHA)* What do you want? Don't—

ALYOSHA: Ivan, I want to—

GRUSHENKA: Alyosha, oh thank you, Ivan Fyodorovich—

ALYOSHA: I've wanted to talk with you—

GRUSHENKA: —come in, you did come, thank you, talk to him, please, he's been asking—

IVAN: *(To* DMITRI*)* Listen. If they convict you. If they send you to Siberia. I've learned who to bribe to help you escape on the way.

DMITRI: You think I did it, don't you.

IVAN: I don't care. You'll have to leave Russia for a long time.

GRUSHENKA: Who's paying?

IVAN: I'm putting up some—

DMITRI: Who's paying? Katya? Katya thinks I did it.

IVAN: Nobody said you did it.

ALYOSHA: Mitya. You didn't.

DMITRI: Really?

ALYOSHA: Really. You did not do it.

(Pause)

IVAN: Dmitri. On the stand, you said you heard your brother's voice, that night. Alyosha's voice. So you didn't kill Father. You said that. What if you'd heard my voice? What would you have done?

DMITRI: I don't know.

*(*IVAN *crosses away.)*

ALYOSHA: Brother, wait! *(To* GRUSHENKA *and* DMITRI*)* Pardon me, please, I have to—

*(*ALYOSHA *pursues* IVAN*.)*

IVAN: You think I'm insane, don't you.

ALYOSHA: What? No. You look ill.

IVAN: Do you know how people go insane?

ALYOSHA: I guess all kinds of ways.

IVAN: Do you think they can see it happening to them?

ALYOSHA: I wouldn't think they could see themselves well enough.

IVAN: Who killed our father?

ALYOSHA: You know who.

IVAN: Smerdyakov? Are you still on that?

ALYOSHA: You know who.

IVAN: So who?

ALYOSHA: I know this: It was not you who killed Father.

IVAN: "Not me"? What do you mean, "not me"?

ALYOSHA: It was not you who killed Father, Ivan. Not you.

(The DEVIL *enters and waves to* IVAN.*)*

IVAN: I know I didn't. I was in Moscow.

ALYOSHA: You've told yourself you're the murderer and no one else. But you didn't do it. You are wrong. You are not the murderer. Do you hear? It was not you!

IVAN: How do you know all that? *(He points at the* DEVIL.*)* You can see Him, too!

ALYOSHA: Who?

IVAN: You can! You can see Him! Are you insane, too?

ALYOSHA: No.

*(*IVAN *looks at the* DEVIL.*)*

IVAN: Do you ever think of the temptation of Jesus in the wilderness?

ALYOSHA: I'm a novice, Ivan. I think about the Temptor all the time.

IVAN: Jesus walks into the wilderness. He walks for days. He walks upright in the sun, casting a long shadow. The shadow matches him stride for stride, slithering over the furrows and gullies in the earth. A couple of weeks into the desert, Jesus notices, now and then, a shape in the corner of his eye. When he turns toward it, away from the sun, his eyes feel a little cooler, his mouth no longer so dry. He feels more comfortable, facing his shadow. A tiny temptation. The first. So he turns and walks again. By the thirtieth day, Jesus' shadow walks upright beside him, matching him stride for stride. A shadow that casts no shadow. A hole in the light of the world. Don't you think they must have walked side by side for days, in silence? To the middle of the open plain. And then they stop, on the fortieth day, as it was written. The wind blows across that plain like the spirit of the world, headlong and howling. A pounding sun. The two of them, standing in the dust. Two visitors in the world. No sweat left in them. Jesus and Satan. Born of the same Creator. Two brothers.

ALYOSHA: You've thought a great deal about our Savior, haven't you?

IVAN: I'm an atheist, Alyosha. I think about God all the time. Do you think Satan ever wanted to say to Jesus, "Why do you get to be the good one? We had the same father. Why do you get to be the one who needs nothing, and I was created to be nothing but a parcel of infinite wants?"

ALYOSHA: Surely his pride would keep him from admitting that.

IVAN: Most days. With most people. But not when he stands in the wilderness, beside his younger brother.

ALYOSHA: I tell you, once and for all, it was not you. Do you hear? God has put it into my heart to tell you this, Ivan, even if you hate me for it. You are not what you think you are.

IVAN: I can't stand prophets and angels. Leave me, please.

ALYOSHA: Brother! If anything happens to you, send for me!

(IVAN *runs away, leaving* ALYOSHA *behind. The* DEVIL *follows* IVAN.)

Scene Six

(The DEVIL *ushers* IVAN *to where* SMERDYAKOV *is sitting. Then he sits and watches them.)*

SMERDYAKOV: Sir. You look unwell.

IVAN: I won't keep you long. See? I'm keeping my coat on.

SMERDYAKOV: Worried about something? The trial?

IVAN: Why should I be worried about the trial?

SMERDYAKOV: I don't see why you have to keep play-acting. Nothing is going to happen to you! Look at his hands shaking—you weren't the one who killed him!

IVAN: I know I wasn't.

SMERDYAKOV: You're sure? Good. Go home, get some rest, you look terrible, Sir.

IVAN: Smerdyakov! Tell me what you did!

SMERDYAKOV: If you're going to stay, take off your coat, the room's overheated.

IVAN: In a minute.

SMERDYAKOV: Would you like some lemonade? It's very refreshing.

IVAN: You stinking bastard! What did you do?

SMERDYAKOV: Well, Ivan, it really was you, when it's all said and done.

IVAN: You're crazy.

SMERDYAKOV: When are you going to stop play-acting? You did it, you were the head killer, I was nothing but your cat's-paw.

IVAN: You killed him?

(SMERDYAKOV *holds out a wad of bills to* IVAN.)

IVAN: Smerdyakov. What have you done.

SMERDYAKOV: Three thousand. It's all there, Sir.

IVAN: God. God! Did you do it alone, with Dmitri, what?

SMERDYAKOV: It was just you and me, Sir, just us, Dmitri's innocent.

IVAN: Why do my hands keep shaking—

SMERDYAKOV: You really didn't know? Do you mean to tell me that you—

IVAN: My lips won't work right—

SMERDYAKOV: But that would mean that I—no, you knew, you must have known, you told me the last time we talked that you knew all along—

IVAN: I didn't, I said maybe I suspected, but—

SMERDYAKOV: I was acting on your explicit—

IVAN: I never—

SMERDYAKOV: But that would mean that—I acted alone! All alone! Me! Just...me...

IVAN: I'm not really seeing you. You're just something in my eye, a shape, you're one of the voices I hear in my head.

SMERDYAKOV: I'm really here. So are you. It's just you and me, and one other.

IVAN: Who? Who's here?

SMERDYAKOV: Well, God, Sir. Sitting behind the walls and judging. Don't look, you can't see him anyway, the world's too bright. Here. The money's all there, take it.

(SMERDYAKOV *puts down the money.* IVAN *picks it up.*)

IVAN: Did you have a real fit, or were you faking?

SMERDYAKOV: Faking, of course. It was all an act.

IVAN: It was an act later, too, in the hospital?

SMERDYAKOV: No, it's funny, I must have convinced myself somehow, because the next day I had a real attack, worst in years, I was out for two days.

IVAN: I'll testify tomorrow, that's what I'll do, and you'll confess.

SMERDYAKOV: They'll say you're delirious. Look at your eyes, they're all yellow—

IVAN: People can judge whether I really put you up to it or whether I just wished it might happen, somehow.

SMERDYAKOV: Why are you doing this? Why are you forsaking me?

IVAN: I ought to kill you right now.

SMERDYAKOV: Ivan! I only did what you wanted!

IVAN: All I ever wanted in the world was justice.

SMERDYAKOV: Our son of a bitch of a father is dead. That's justice.

IVAN: And Dmitri? Where's the justice for him?

SMERDYAKOV: Dmitri wanted him dead. Another night, he might have done it himself. Even Alyosha thought he was evil, he could have stood guard over Father, but he was too busy getting holy. You wanted him dead. Everyone benefits from his death but me. I'm out of a job. And all you can think about is how to save Dmitri by sacrificing me, because you've only ever thought of me as some kind of insect, not a human being with a soul like anyone.

IVAN: Why did you kill him?

SMERDYAKOV: Dmitri was running away. I'd prepared him, rehearsed him in our secret knock, told him the money was under the pillow. Everybody knew something had to be done! I thought I'd been put there for a reason! I felt a craving, like a thirst, like a dry ache down my throat—

IVAN: A craving for what?

SMERDYAKOV: For everything to be over. Haven't you ever felt that? Don't people ever? Am I as different from a human being as that?

(IVAN *shakes his head "no".*)

SMERDYAKOV: Is that a no? No, what? No, you've never felt that? No, I'm not a human being?

IVAN: I've felt that.

SMERDYAKOV: Never mind, I don't need your answer, to hell with your answer. I got up and went to the door. I gave the secret knock. Father shouted Grushenka's name. He opened the door, right that instant, didn't even wait for an answer. He must have loved her a lot, somehow. When he saw it was only me, he turned his back. He was always doing that. On the third blow I felt his skull give way.

IVAN: We'll go to the police. We'll confess.

SMERDYAKOV: You won't go.

IVAN: I've got evidence. I've got the money.

SMERDYAKOV: You can't prove it's Father's, you might as well keep it. You can't prove anything.

IVAN: I'll kill you right now!

SMERDYAKOV: Fine. Kill me. Kill me now! *(Pause)* I used to think you were brave, Ivan. When you told me there is no God, and no need for goodness, that anything is true, and everything is permitted—why did you teach me those things!—I thought, my brother is a strong man. He curses God in the face. I must have known God existed back then, or you couldn't have seemed so brave.

IVAN: And now you believe in God again. That's why you're giving the money—

SMERDYAKOV: No. If he did exist, you'd never have said those things. You wouldn't have the nerve. He doesn't exist. And you won't testify.

IVAN: You'll see.

SMERDYAKOV: You won't waste your life for a meaningless gesture. You're too proud. You hate to bow to anyone. Just like Father. You know, of all of us, you resemble him the most.

IVAN: I used to think you were stupid. You're not stupid.

SMERDYAKOV: That was you being proud, Sir. You have the money? You have your coat? Wait…show it to me one more time.

(IVAN holds out the money. SMERDYAKOV looks at it.)

SMERDYAKOV: All right, now go.

(SMERDYAKOV lies down again as IVAN crosses away. The DEVIL walks behind him.)

Scene Seven

(The DEVIL *taps* IVAN *on the shoulder.* IVAN *yells and shies away.)*

IVAN: Disappear, would you?

DEVIL: I've got nowhere else to go. I'm your hallucination, Ivan.

IVAN: You're nothing! You're nothing but what I think of you!

DEVIL: But Ivan. That's how you feel about everyone.

IVAN: Look, I'd love to talk, but I'm delirious at the moment.

DEVIL: I'm sorry. As symptoms go, I'm not the worst company. I know, you were expecting something profound, right, something beautiful in a Byronic sort of way. I'm doing my best, but I am here on vacation.

IVAN: The Earth is a vacation for you?

DEVIL: Oh, yes. I love how real it all is. And the clarity! On the plane where I dwell? Chaos. You know what I did today? I went to the children's hospital and got myself a smallpox vaccination. I was so happy I gave a donation.

IVAN: Smallpox vaccination?

DEVIL: If I can take human form, I can catch a human disease. Can't be too careful.

IVAN: I don't remember ever thinking that. Odd.

DEVIL: Oh, no, listen, all it is: I'm a dream you're having. Don't you ever get new ideas in your dreams? I love dreaming. I come here just to have a body so my body can dream.

IVAN: You can't dream...where you're from?

DEVIL: Of course not, Ivan. I'm from Hell. You know
what I'd love to do this trip? Go to church and light
a candle. *(He does so.)* I'd love to believe in God.
Wouldn't you?

IVAN: Do you mean to say the Devil doesn't believe in
God?

DEVIL: How shall I put this….

IVAN: Is there a God or not?

DEVIL: Who wants to know?

IVAN: Answer me! Is there a God!

DEVIL: I don't know.

IVAN: What am I doing? You don't know? I'm arguing
with a figment of my own imagination.

DEVIL: I can prove that I don't exist. Shall I? Let's say
this candle—this light, this illumination—is God. A
force of warmth and a power of destruction. All right?
Now. Let's say that I, standing here, represent the
material world.

IVAN: Given you don't exist, it's a stretch.

DEVIL: —separate from God, different in nature. All
right? Now—

IVAN: Do I represent something?

DEVIL: You stand for yourself. It's a stretch. So there's
you: separate from the world, separate from God.
Observing. So. God, World, You: your image of the
universe. Now. Tell me what's behind me.

IVAN: Nothing.

DEVIL: In a way you're right. Look again.

IVAN: I can't see anything, besides, it's dark.

DEVIL: Is it?

IVAN: You're standing in front of the candle, you fool, you make a better door than a window, you're casting a shadow.

DEVIL: Yes. And the shadow in question would be... me. A hole, as an eloquent young man once said, in the light of the world. Ivan Fyodorovich, if you think that the world is a solid thing, distant from God, that the world is a door not a window, a door to nowhere... why, then the very light by which you see the world must cast behind it a huge black thing the shape of the world and many times as large, which you have named Satan. And which wears a face...that you know well.

IVAN: How can I make you go away?

DEVIL: Stop believing in me.

IVAN: I don't believe in you!

DEVIL: Who are you talking to?

IVAN: I am talking to nobody! I am talking to myse....

(Pause. The DEVIL *holds out the candle.)*

DEVIL: When you come to believe that the world is the source of its own illumination, that you are in the world, and God is, too, then the world will be a window, clear as glass, and then there will be no shadow, because everything will be made of light.

*(*IVAN *takes the candle and looks at the flame. Then he smothers it in his hand.)*

IVAN: Get out.

DEVIL: So be it. You come, too.

IVAN: Where are we going?

DEVIL: Dmitri's trial.

IVAN: What?

KATYA: Ivan!

JUDGE: *(Whose horns are gone)* I said, are you all right?

KATYA: Can't you see he's ill!

JUDGE: Mister Karamazov, am I right in understanding you to say that an apparition of Satan has visited you in your room?

(IVAN looks around, disoriented at the others who are there.)

IVAN: I said that?

JUDGE: You have interrupted the procedings, Mister Karamazov—

IVAN: That's not what I came here to say—

KATYA: He is ill, Your Honor—

IVAN: —what I came here to confess—

ALYOSHA: Ivan! Don't damn yourself!

IVAN: Too late! I have come to give evidence against myself and my—I was going to say my brother—

NELYUDOV: Your brother Dmitri?

IVAN: My brother Smerdyakov, but no—

NELYUDOV: We have already heard—

IVAN: No though, not my brother. Somehow? My son...

JUDGE: What are you saying, Mister Karamazov.

IVAN: I seem, without knowing it, to be the father of Smerdyakov's soul!

(Pause)

NELYUDOV: Mister Karamazov. The man Smerdyakov is dead. He hanged himself. Out of grief for his dead master, we believe.

IVAN: Out of guilt.

NELYUDOV: He left no message.

IVAN: Smerdyakov and I killed my father.

KATYA: No, Ivan!

ALYOSHA: Stop—

IVAN: I gave him the idea.

KATYA: Your Honor, this man is delirious—

JUDGE: Order.

IVAN: He gave me his ability to act.

KATYA: I will not permit this!

DMITRI: Now, yes, now they come—

JUDGE: Order!

IVAN: Too late!

KATYA: Your Honor!!

DMITRI: They circle downward, hear the wings—

KATYA: Your Honor, I will not let this good man perjure himself—

DMITRI: Now they land—

GRUSHENKA: Your Honor, this is jealousy, spite—

IVAN: Katya, please, let me—

KATYA: Your Honor, I demand that I testify again—

DMITRI: The Furies—

KATYA: Your Honor, I have a piece of evidence—

DMITRI: My Furies are here—

KATYA: I have a letter written to me by Dmitri Karamazov.

DMITRI: It is finished.

(The lights fade.)

Scene Eight

(A small crowd of PRISONERS *is strewn across the floor, sleeping or resting, hidden in their coats.* DMITRI *is kneeling.* ALYOSHA, GRUSHENKA, *and* FENYA *are nearby.)*

DMITRI: I can't do it.

ALYOSHA: It's done, Mitya, the plans are in place, the guards are bribed—

DMITRI: I have to see Katya. I have to talk to Ivan.

ALYOSHA: He's terribly ill, Mitya, I can't even find out where they took him, he's not in the hospital—

DMITRI: And Katya? I'm sorry, Grushka, but I can't live without her forgiveness, I know I don't deserve it, but—

GRUSHENKA: She destroyed you.

DMITRI: She brought down my punishment. It's just, whatever happens to me is just.

ALYOSHA: Twenty years in the mines! Mitya, you're not guilty.

DMITRI: I'm guilty of my whole life. No one but me. I've blamed my Karamazov blood long enough.

ALYOSHA: Stop trying to accept this injustice! Mitya, it's too heavy a cross. You want to make up for everything and suffer for everyone all at once, but you can't. As it is you have to leave Russia forever and go someplace like America, isn't that penance enough?

*(*KATYA *enters and watches them.)*

KATYA: Forgive me.

GRUSHENKA: Come to see the fruits of your labor?

KATYA: I came to be punished. Not by you.

DMITRI: Grusha. Can't you forgive her?

GRUSHENKA: Who are we to forgive each other?

KATYA: She's right not to forgive me. I like her for that.

DMITRI: Grusha, look at her. Can't you see she's ashamed?

GRUSHENKA: (Smiling terribly) Never be ashamed.

ALYOSHA: Just a moment. Katya. Do you know what has happened to Ivan?

KATYA: I ordered him carried to my house. I'm nursing him there.

ALYOSHA: That is a great act of charity.

KATYA: No. I'm doing it because I love him.

ALYOSHA: I think that's what charity means.

DMITRI: What was he trying to do at my trial? What did it mean?

KATYA: That was an act of charity. Pure charity. It put me to shame. I knew in that moment I loved him.

DMITRI: Charity. So he thought I did it. He was trying to save his brother.

ALYOSHA: Mitya, no. I think Ivan was trying to join the world.

FENYA: Listen to them.

GRUSHENKA: What?

FENYA: They think they're explaining Ivan Fyodorovich and all they can do is explain themselves.

KATYA: I've put Ivan's plan in motion. The money is paid, the guards are bribed.

(GRUSHENKA seizes KATYA's hand. She pulls it to her lips and gives it three kisses.)

GRUSHENKA: He wanted to talk to you. Talk to him. Talk to each other!

DMITRI: Please. Forgive me?

KATYA: When we were in love, before all this—when I danced in your arms I worshipped you, I would look up and think, how can I ever be worthy of this man. And now—

DMITRI: Do you believe I killed my father?

KATYA: When I said that, I hated you, my hatred made me believe whatever I said. No, I came here—I always meant to tell you what I thought you were.

DMITRI: Tell.

KATYA: I never quite knew till I got to know all of you, Ivan, you, Alyosha, all you Karamazovs. I've never met anyone—anyone—who wanted so much to be good.

DMITRI: I'll love you all my life—

KATYA: I'll love you forever.

DMITRI: Doomed to it.

FENYA: What a performance.

GRUSHENKA: Is it true?

ALYOSHA: They want it to be.

FENYA: I wouldn't worry, then.

KATYA: *(To* GRUSHENKA*)* He wanted to be reborn. For you. The door's open.

DMITRI: I won't run from my punishment. I've run all my life.

GRUSHENKA: Mitya. I think you should do it.

DMITRI: No, Grushka, I'll survive, I'll come back, I'll find you, I love you, don't—

GRUSHENKA: Here.

*(*GRUSHENKA *holds out a sheaf of papers, which* DMITRI *takes.)*

DMITRI: What—?

GRUSHENKA: They're your notes. For your debt.

DMITRI: But—

GRUSHENKA: I forgive them. Your debt to your father is discharged. You're free.

DMITRI: Why?

GRUSHENKA: I don't need them anymore. Not where I'm going.

DMITRI: Where are you going?

GRUSHENKA: That depends.

DMITRI: On what?

GRUSHENKA: Where you're going. Away from Russia, we won't know the language. So we won't have to talk to anyone. And no one will know who we are. So we won't have to be anyone. It could be good.

ALYOSHA: She's right, Mitya. It would be like a vow of silence. It would be a pilgrimage into the world.

(GRUSHENKA *and* DMITRI *embrace.*)

CONSTABLE: *(Off)* Visitors out!

KATYA: Goodbye, all of you—

ALYOSHA: *(Embracing* GRUSHENKA*)* Sister—care for Mitya—

DMITRI: *(To* KATYA*)* Care for Ivan—

KATYA: He will recover. We will work to put his thoughts into action. We will change Russia beyond recognition.

(GRUSHENKA *and* FENYA *embrace.*)

CONSTABLE: *(Off)* Visitors out!

ALYOSHA: One moment—

CONSTABLE: *(Off)* Prisoners! Time to go!

ALYOSHA: I...I have something to say. I don't know
when we'll see each other again. When I leave this
place, I'll begin a pilgrimage. Pilgrims pass through
our monastery all the time, carrying icons—clear
across Russia, some of them. For blessing, and a little
protection from the wind, I think, and to help them
to remember why they walk. You will be my icons.
Whatever I do when I walk through the world, I
will do in your presence. We're all leaving here on a
pilgrimage. Let's carry each other. Until we meet again.
And we'll tell each other every place all of us have
been.

(KATYA, GRUSHENKA, *and* FENYA *go.*)

DMITRI: Brother.

ALYOSHA: Brother.

(DMITRI *and* ALYOSHA *embrace.* DMITRI *goes.* ALYOSHA
starts to follow him.)

FIRST PRISONER: Hey.

SECOND PRISONER: *(Faintly)* Hey.

FIRST PRISONER: Father Karamazov—

SECOND PRISONER: Father Karamazov?

FIRST PRISONER: —over here?

ALYOSHA: I am not a priest.

SECOND PRISONER: Please?

FIRST PRISONER: This man and me, we're for Siberia.
We've been this road before. We'll never see it.

ALYOSHA: What do you want.

FIRST PRISONER: Guards beat him bad.

ALYOSHA: Do you want a doctor?

SECOND PRISONER: Whatever you can spare.

FIRST PRISONER: He wants someone to bless him.

(ALYOSHA *kneels by the* SECOND PRISONER *and helps him sit up and uncover his head and his face. The face is* FYODOR KARAMAZOV's.)

(ALYOSHA *holds out his hands, palms up. The old man takes them.* ALYOSHA *bows his head to the floor before the old man. He rises.*)

SECOND PRISONER: And whatever you can spare.

(ALYOSHA *takes off his cassock, drapes it around the* PRISONER, *bends and kisses his head. He stands.*)

THIRD PRISONER: Father Karamazov?

MORE PRISONERS: Father? Over here.

FOURTH PRISONER: Father Karamazov.

ALL: Father? Father? Father?

END OF PLAY

www.ingramcontent.com/pod-product-compliance
Lightning Source LLC
Chambersburg PA
CBHW070015110426
42741CB00034B/1880